ITALIAN
FOOD
SAFARI

ITALIAN FOOD SAFARI

A delicious celebration of the Italian kitchen

MAEVE O'MEARA
WITH GUY GROSSI

hardie grant books
MELBOURNE • LONDON

SBS

CONTENTS

'For Italians, every meal, no matter how simple, is a celebration or a feast … It's about being together and enjoying something special. If you've got time together and it's a family table, then it's a special day.' Guy Grossi

INTRODUCTION

To be born into the Italian realm is to be part of a lifetime feast – an existence punctuated by the best produce of the season prepared with love and passion. This is a world away from the nuclear family and the lone cook labouring away in the kitchen – it's warm, welcoming and loud. Three and sometimes four generations gather together, the women laughing as they go about creating magic in the kitchen, the men often tending a wood-fired oven outside.

Rituals dominate Italian culinary life – events that bring families and communities together. In late summer it's the bottling of the season's ripest tomatoes; in winter it's preserving every part of a pig as sausages, prosciutto and salami.

The work involved is usually intense and calls for a large number of people to join in. And that means even more food to keep everyone going. And so, the recipes that have been passed down through the family are lovingly prepared over and over again in a way that keeps the culture of the village alive – even half a world away from the source.

Keeping culture and traditions alive is fundamental to Italians – the hunting and gathering; cheese-making, preserving and baking; and commemoration of holy days are the staff of daily life.

We have been lucky to share in the rituals and gather recipes from people hailing from Italy's many varied regions, from Sicily to the mountainous border of Austria. And to share, as well, in the wonderful culinary wisdom of many sayings and strictures – precious gems you can only gather in the fragrant steam of the kitchen.

Please read, cook from and enjoy our Italian Food Safari – a journey into a delicious and generous world.

TOMATO DAY

If Italy has a colour, it's red – for tomatoes in all their glorious incarnations, in pastas, pizzas, ragu and salads, and preserved in passata to be used through the year.

It's intriguing to realise that tomatoes were only introduced to Italy from South America in the sixteenth century. Their Italian name is '*pomodoro*' – literally 'golden apple', a fruit prized for its combination of sweetness and acidity and its incredible versatility.

Guy Grossi remembers his dad spending the few hours he wasn't at his restaurant out in his garden, lovingly tending his tomato crop. 'My father used to grow tomatoes that smelt and tasted like a real tomato – with the intensity of flavour that can only be achieved when home-grown and organic.'

Italians are fussy about everything in food, but especially tomatoes. Frank Bonfante has sold home-grown and commercial tomatoes for forty years and says many Italian buyers smell their tomatoes first. The best aroma equals the best flavour – and it's especially important to smell your tomatoes when making passata, says Maria Cipri. 'One bad one can ruin the lot,' she warns.

Passata is essentially a puree of tomatoes and is made by families from all over Italy, but especially from the south where the tomato rules. The homemade sauce tastes pure, sweet and full of sunshine and gives a special magic to every dish.

You need a big family to wash and cut boxes and boxes of tomatoes. Many families buy up to fifty boxes to ensure their supply of passata through the year – which might be three or four bottles per week.

The methods for making passata differ slightly from region to region, and family to family, but generally the tomatoes are heated to boiling point then passed through a special crushing device with a sieve that removes the skins and seeds. These are squeezed to release as much flavour as possible.

In Daniel Airo-Farulla's family, he remembers each person having a special job – the grown-ups on the machine that removes skins and seeds, and the kids carefully placing one leaf of basil in each bottle before the sauce is added.

Once the bottles are filled and capped (many families use long-neck beer bottles that have been circulating for decades), the bottles are placed in a cavernous drum

Definition of catastrophe
in an Italian household –
running out of tomato sauce
before summer comes!

that sits over a large gas ring. Hessian is placed on the bottom as well as in between the bottles to cushion them, and the drum is filled with water and brought to the boil to sterilise the bottles. Maria Cipri and her family learnt to leave the bottles cooling in the water overnight, because if you remove them too early they can crack.

Many Italian friends say they used to dread tomato day when they were growing up because it was always a hot time of year and they would rather have been at the beach. But now they treasure it. Carmelo Cipri always looked forward to it. 'There's something about producing food for the family – and with the family,' he says. 'The flavour goes from your tastebuds right to your heart!'

The Cipri family's tomato day tradition began forty-five years ago when Severio and Maria bottled tomatoes in the summer of their first year in Australia. It was important for them to continue the tradition, and they've done so every year since then. Their immediate family and friends now number around thirty and everyone pitches in for a few hours' work before a big lunch featuring some of their beautiful tomato sauce. A long table is set up and many courses are served along with Severio's homemade wine.

Tomato day is a symbol of culture in both Italy and Australia. Intriguingly, many Italian Australian families say their families back home have stopped tomato day as it's so much work, but in Australia it is still going strong.

NAPOLETANA SAUCE

CARMELO CIPRI

3 tablespoons
 extra-virgin olive oil
1 garlic clove, finely chopped
1 kg tinned Italian tomatoes,
 or fresh tomatoes, peeled
salt and pepper
10 basil leaves

Italian cuisine is nothing without this building block – the simplest sauce in the world – wonderful in slow braises or just served with pasta. (Carmelo boils pasta – 100 g of dried pasta per person – until it is three-quarters cooked, then drains it, adds it to the sauce and continues to cook it in the sauce for another 2–3 minutes before adding the basil.)

Heat the oil in a saucepan over medium heat and add the garlic. Fry briefly then add the tomato. Bring to the boil, then reduce the heat to a low simmer and cook for 20 minutes. Season with salt and pepper and tear over the basil at the last minute.

Serves 4

Se piove e viene il sole, fagiolini e pomodori. (If it rains and the sun shines there will be green beans and tomatoes.)'

PARMIGIANA DI MELANZANE
EGGPLANT PARMIGIANA

FROM ROSA MATTO

3 large eggplants
salt
plain flour
4 eggs, beaten
olive oil

SUGO
80 ml olive oil
1 onion, finely chopped
1 garlic clove, chopped
750 ml tomato puree (Rosa
    uses homemade passata)
    or an 800 g tin Italian
    tomatoes, or 12 very ripe
    tomatoes, peeled and
    chopped
salt and pepper
½ bunch basil leaves,
    chopped, plus extra leaves
    for layering
250 g bocconcini or fresh
    mozzarella, sliced
100 g parmesan, grated

As a young teacher posted to the outback, Rosa Matto began to intro-duce good Italian home cooking to her fellow staff and local families. She later set up her own cooking school and has taught legions of people to appreciate Italian food. Recipes like this one are from Campania, where her family comes from.

This is a favourite picnic dish, and sometimes Rosa uses zucchini instead of eggplant. It is a little time-consuming to prepare, though the result is always worthwhile and the dish feeds lots of people as part of a spread. (If you also plan to serve the dish at room temperature at a picnic, the recipe is best made without bocconcini as it hardens on cooling.)

Slice the eggplant no thicker than 1 cm. Sprinkle the slices with salt, stack in a colander and weight down with a heavy object. Leave for 1 hour. Pat the slices dry and lightly coat in flour. Dip into the beaten egg, shaking off the excess, and fry in hot oil until golden brown on each side. Drain on paper towel.

To make the *sugo*, heat the oil and fry the onion and garlic until soft. Add the tomato and bring to the boil. Cook until lightly thickened. Season to taste and add half of the basil.

Preheat the oven to 180°C. Smear the bottom of a baking dish with *sugo* then add a layer of eggplant. Dot with slices of bocconcini, a sprinkling of parmesan and a few torn basil leaves. Continue to layer until you have used up the eggplant, and finish with *sugo* topped with cheese.

Bake for 20–25 minutes, until the top is golden. Allow to rest for 10 minutes or so. To serve, lift off layers rather than cutting a wedge.

Serves 6

'Approximate amount of
sauce per family per week:
3 to 4 litre bottles.'

SPAGHETTI NERA
SICILIAN BLACK SPAGHETTI

FROM CLAUDE BASILE

3 cuttlefish, cleaned, plus
   1 large or 2 small ink sacs
2 tablespoons olive oil
1 onion, diced
1 small red chilli, sliced
4 garlic cloves, finely chopped
800 g tin Italian tomatoes
750 ml tomato puree
   (or homemade passata
   if available)
140 g tomato paste
salt and pepper
1 kg dried spaghetti

Claude learnt this recipe for spaghetti with black sauce when he joined his grandfather to fish off the Western Australian coast. It's basically a *Napoletana* sauce with cuttlefish and their ink, which adds a dark iodine taste of the sea.

Cut the cuttlefish bodies and tentacles into short, thin strips. Heat a frying pan over low heat and add the cuttlefish without oil. Cook, stirring, until the juices evaporate, then transfer to a bowl.

Add the oil to the frying pan and brown the onion, chilli and garlic. Add the tomatoes, tomato puree and tomato paste and season with salt and pepper. Before the mixture comes to the boil, squeeze in the cuttlefish ink, then add the cuttlefish and simmer for 30 minutes.

Cook the spaghetti in salted boiling water, then toss with the cuttlefish sauce.

Serves 8–10

'Food, and to share your table, are the most precious gifts that you can offer.' Pietro Demaio

COZZE ALLA SICILIANA

BRAISED MUSSELS WITH TOMATO, CHILLI AND OLIVES

FROM GUY GROSSI

200 ml olive oil
1 garlic clove, thinly sliced
chopped red chilli to taste
400 ml tomato puree
200 ml white wine
pinch of chopped fresh
    (or dried) oregano
sea salt
freshly ground black pepper
1 kg mussels, cleaned and
    de-bearded
½ cup chopped flat-leaf
    parsley
handful of basil leaves
100 g black olives, stoned

Very fresh mussels are essential to this dish – when they open they release all their lovely sea water into the sauce, and as you're eating this you should taste the ocean.

Heat the olive oil in a heavy-based saucepan and sauté the garlic and chilli until lightly softened. Add the tomato puree, wine and oregano and season with salt and pepper. Add the mussels and cover with a lid. Cook for about 3 minutes, shaking the pan occasionally, until the mussels open. Scatter with the herbs and olives and serve immediately.

Serves 4

'Never eat so much that you cannot accept food offered by a friend.'

PRESERVING

Preserving is the most ancient of food traditions. In the Italian world it means being able to enjoy fruit and vegetables out of season, as well as securing a good source of protein from meat, salami and sausages through to salted anchovies and chunks of tuna in oil. It is said that an Italian cellar can withstand any major disaster and last to the next Ice Age!

The rhythm of the seasons dictates what's on the table. And the garage is the centre of the food universe for many families – the preserving workshop. Danny Russo gives us the calendar of his childhood:

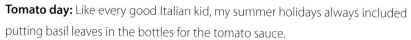

Tomato day: Like every good Italian kid, my summer holidays always included putting basil leaves in the bottles for the tomato sauce.

Cherry picking: After tomato day, the reward for the family and cousins was to go to the country and pick cherries for the day.

Wine day: No choice in the matter. I helped my dad and uncles to make their pride and joy each autumn. We called it *Chateau di Five Dock* (a suburb filled with many Italian families).

Mushroom picking: An amazing day in the pine forests with all the cousins – freezing but great! We preserved enough mushrooms for the year.

Salami and prosciutto day: Wintertime. It just so happened that the perfect time was smack in the middle of our school holidays. My dad and uncle would do the butchery and my mum and auntie would do the seasoning and spices.

Bread and pasta: A weekly job.

Nino Zoccali says you could tell the time of year by what was coming out of the garden, what was on the plate and what was being made or preserved. 'We had tomato sauce and pickled summer vegetables at the end of summer; we made homemade wine from Dad's vineyard and preserved olives a hundred different ways in early autumn; killed the pig for sausages and *salumi* and preserved vegetables in winter; roasted baby goat and ate fennel salad in spring. Dad is a keen hunter as well, so during hunting season the wild ducks in our district usually had a pretty challenging time of it!'

'*Cu si sposa e cuntentu na notti;
cu mazza u maiali e cuntentu
tuttu l'annu!* (He who marries
is happy for one night; he who
kills the pig is happy all year!)'

A nonna from Ferruzzano, Calabria,
speaking with Pietro Demaio

A pioneer in promoting some of the secrets passed on through Italian families is the inspiring Pietro Demaio. His parents were from Calabria and he believed that many of the skills for preserving produce were in danger of being lost. So he collected the wisdom of many Italians in a book about preserving that's become a bestseller.

As well as the joy of being self-sufficient, says Pietro, the proof is in the flavour – of everything from home-cured pancetta to tuna. 'The taste difference between the commercial product and what you can make yourself is ... truly like night and day. The only warning is that once you've tasted something like fresh tuna you've pre-served yourself, with no metallic edge to it, then you're spoilt for everything else!'

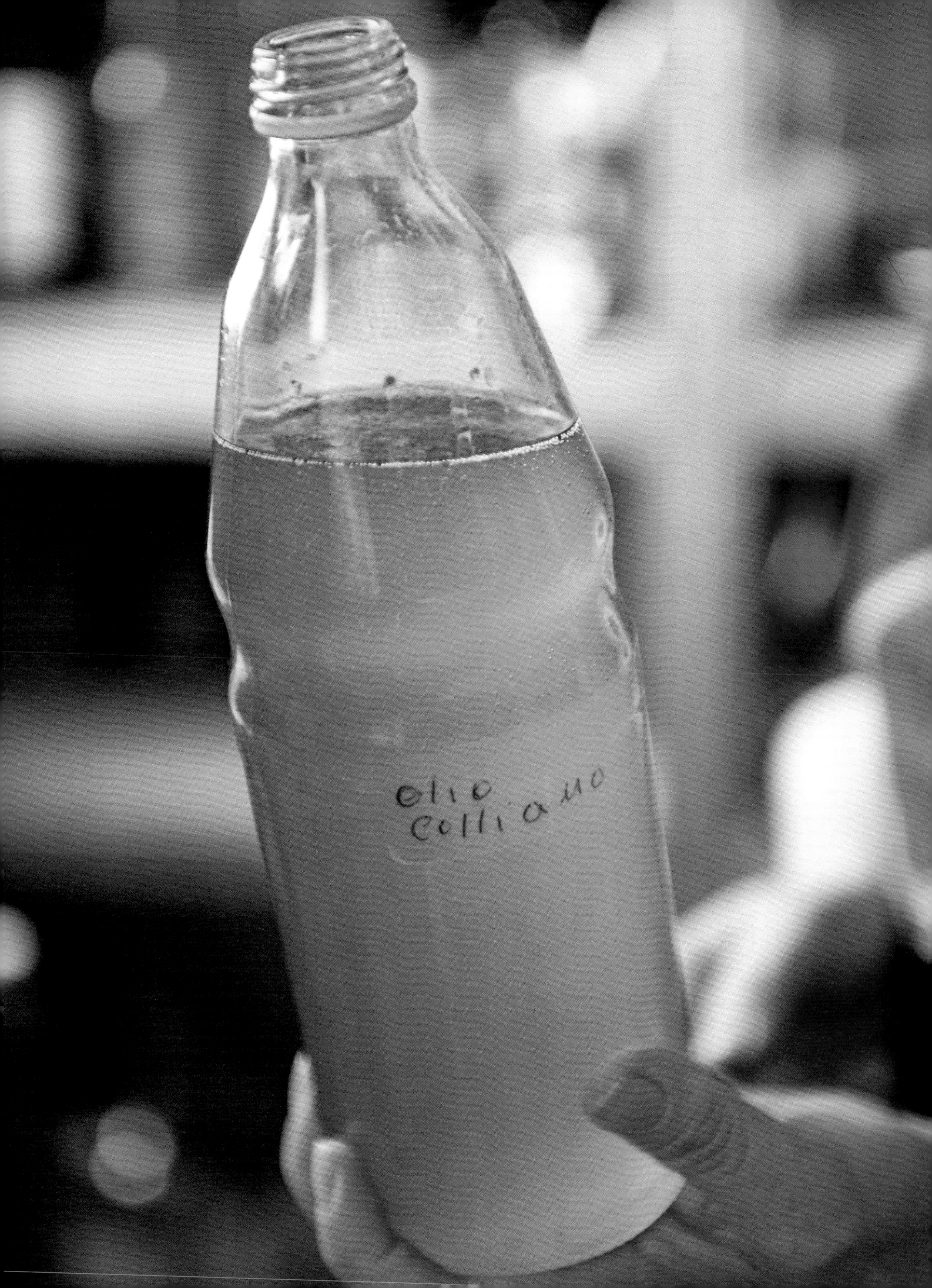
olio
colliano

TONNO SOTT'OLIO
TUNA IN OIL

FROM PIETRO DEMAIO

blue- or yellow-fin tuna, sliced
    into 10 cm chunks including
    skin and bones
salt
good-quality light olive oil
garlic cloves, cut into slivers
bay leaves
lemons, sliced
red chillies, sliced

If you are lucky enough to come across a large quantity of fresh tuna (even 50 kilograms), then this is a great way to use it. You'll have a long supply of preserved tuna, and the difference between this and what's available in tins is like the comparison between fresh and tinned asparagus. It's life changing!

Weigh the tuna pieces and put into a large pot. For every 1 kg of fish, add 120 g of salt. Cover with water and bring to a simmer. Cook for 3 hours over low heat. This is best done outside on a barbecue so the smell doesn't take over the house.

Drain the cooked tuna pieces and lay on tea towels. Leave to dry and cool overnight.

The next morning, remove the skin and bones and break the fish into smaller pieces that will fit inside wide-necked jars. Pour a little oil into the base of your jars. Add the pieces of tuna and pack down firmly. Add a few slivers of garlic, slices of lemon, bay leaves and slices of chilli to each jar as desired. Cover the tuna with oil and put the lids on the jars.

To sterilise the jars, stand them in a large pot and fill with water to just beneath the lids. Boil for at least 30 minutes, then leave to cool in the water. Leave for at least 1 month before eating.

'Home preserved food will vary from year to year and family to family, as each family produces its own special variation – literally preserving part of their family and cultural history in each jar.' Pietro Demaio

BACCALA MANTECATO

SALT-COD PASTE

FROM BEPPI POLESE

600 g salt cod
⅓ cup finely chopped
    flat-leaf parsley
⅓ cup finely chopped
    celery leaves
pinch of finely chopped chives
4 garlic cloves, finely chopped
6 anchovy fillets, finely
    chopped
freshly ground black pepper
    or dried chilli flakes
juice of 2 lemons
500 ml extra-virgin olive oil

polenta (page 31)

Dried salted cod from the cold waters of Scandinavia is a staple in many European countries, adored for its white flesh that can morph into hundreds of dishes. Beppi Polese has been serving this clever starter in his restaurant since the late 1950s. The salty fish is whipped up with herbs, garlic, lemon and oil into a rich, creamy sauce, and it is all done in a mix-master! It is delicious served with grilled polenta. Just begin soaking the cod two days in advance.

Soak the cod in cold water for 2 days, changing the water 3 times a day.

Bring a saucepan of water to the boil and add the drained cod, boiling for 3 minutes. Drain and leave to cool briefly.

Pick the cod flesh from the skin and bones and place back in the saucepan with 1 litre of fresh water and bring to the boil. Boil for 20 minutes, or until the water reduces to 500 ml. Drain the cod, reserving the cooking water, and leave to cool.

Put the cod, herbs, garlic, anchovies and pepper or chilli to taste into the bowl of an electric mixer with a whisk attachment (alternatively, you could use electric hand beaters). Begin whisking and slowly add the lemon juice, followed by the cod cooking water. Gradually drizzle in the oil and continue whisking for approximately 20 minutes, until the mixture is fluffy.

Serve with grilled polenta.

Serves 4

'Fill your glass when it is empty,
empty it when it's full, never leave
it empty, never leave it full.'

CRACKED GREEN OLIVES

FROM LINA VERRILLI AND PAT D'ONOFRIO

3 kg freshly picked,
    unblemished green olives
250 ml extra-virgin olive oil
1 tablespoon salt
5 garlic cloves, finely chopped
2 tablespoons lemon pepper
2 tablespoons dried oregano
2 tablespoons fennel seeds
dried chilli flakes to taste

This is a simple method for curing green olives. The olives have a mellow flavour and a slight crunch, like blanched vegetables. They're incredibly more-ish; you won't look at green olives in the same way again.

To know if green olives are ripe for curing, cut around an olive and twist the two halves as if opening a peach – the stone should come away easily from the flesh. You'll find the best olives in autumn.

Crack the olives on a solid surface using a mallet or a small beer bottle and remove the stones. Immediately drop the cracked, stoned olives into a bucket of water to stop them from browning.

When all the olives are in the bucket, top it up with water to about 7 cm from the top. Place a dinner plate on top of the olives to keep them fully submerged. After approximately 2 hours, drain off the water and replace with fresh water. Repeat this draining and refilling every 2 hours for the first day, then 2 times a day for the next 4–5 days, or until the olives are no longer bitter. Some olives can take up to 10 days.

Drain the olives in a colander, squeezing out as much water as possible. Place in a large bowl and add the oil, salt, garlic and spices and mix well. Taste for seasoning.

Put on top of grilled crusty bread for a sensational olive bruschetta, or add to your favourite salads, antipasti, sandwiches and focaccias. These olives will keep in the refrigerator for up to 3 weeks, but can also be preserved by packing them into sterilised jars and covering with more oil.

THE CELLAR

The cellar under Franca Norris' country home is a snapshot of the Italian year in bottled form. There are neat bottles of passata and many jars of wild mushrooms in oil; *giardinera* (mixed pickled vegetables); and olives. From the beams overhead hang prosciutto and salami.

This was the house Franca grew up in and moved into with her husband and children when her parents moved to a smaller house. 'We really have inherited the cellar like the family jewels, but more importantly, like the family cookbook. It really is my seasonal pantry in which we lovingly hang our prosciutto and salami or put our bottles and jars on the shelves after each harvest, and smile as the striking colours of the preserves stand out begging to be used for a rich pasta sauce or antipasto platter when family and friends arrive for dinner.

'The cellar creates an emotional bond for me and my family. The memories of a hot day bottling tomato passata, or a family picnic after foraging for *funghi* in the forest, are a reminder of the joy and work that brings everyone together to do their bit, and are all stored down in the cellar for another season.

'As a child, Mum would ask me to collect a jar of olives or a salami if people arrived and I do remember thinking how heavy the trap door was and … Oh!, the beautiful aroma that would rise in the air as I stepped down and ever so carefully held those jars and climbed back up the steps. I used to love sitting on the steps while Dad would entertain his brothers with a taste of the new wine out of the barrel, or some *nocino* [walnut liqueur]. I always got a try.'

POLENTA

6 cups (1½ litres) water
2 teaspoons salt
1 bay leaf
1¾ cups yellow polenta
3 tablespoons butter

Polenta (corn meal) is a glorious, golden carbohydrate adored in the north of Italy, where it's often the centrepiece of a meal. In Abruzzo it's served *a la tavola* – cooked in a big pot, spread out on a table and topped with ragu. In Lombardia it's served firm with gorgonzola or sprinkled with sugar for dessert. For a richer, tastier dish, make the polenta using chicken stock and stir through thinly sliced strips of salami, grated pecorino cheese and finely chopped parsley, thyme and rosemary, and for softer polenta, use milk and a little cream.

Bring the water to a boil in a large, heavy-based saucepan. Add the salt and bay leaf to the water. Gradually sift the polenta through your fingers and into the pan, stirring constantly with a wooden spoon or a whisk. Reduce the heat to low and continue to stir until the polenta is smooth and thick and pulls away from the sides of the pan, about 20 minutes. Turn off the heat. Remove the bay leaf. Add the butter. Polenta can be served immediately or poured evenly into a lightly oiled baking tray to set. Once the polenta has set it can be sliced into batons to serve. The batons can also be lightly pan-fried in olive oil, or grilled until golden brown.

Serves 4–6

'A cucina piccola fa la casa grande. (A small kitchen can make a grand house.)'

CARCIOFI SOTT'OLIO
ARTICHOKES IN OIL

FROM PIETRO DEMAIO

2 litres white-wine vinegar
2 kg small artichokes
1 litre water
8 garlic cloves, peeled,
   plus extra for the jars
5 bay leaves, plus extra for
   the jars
3 cloves
handful of black peppercorns
1 tablespoon salt
sprigs of oregano
olive oil

One winter, grab a friend, buy a box of artichokes and prepare this preserve together. It's easy and fun, and the result is plenty of artichokes to add to pizzas, pastas and salads (and to eat straight from the jar!) for the next year.

The best artichokes to use are the smallest ones. Pietro flavours these artichokes with garlic, bay leaves and oregano, but garlic, mint and chilli is another delicious combination.

Prepare a bowl of water with a dash of the vinegar. Remove the dark outer leaves from the artichokes until you reach the pale inner leaves that feel tender to touch. Trim the stems and cut off the tops of the leaves, exposing the soft heart. As each artichoke is ready, drop it into the bowl of water (the vinegar stops them from discolouring).

Put the vinegar, water, garlic cloves, bay leaves, cloves, peppercorns and salt into a pot and bring to the boil. Add the artichokes. Return the liquid to the boil and cook the artichokes for 5–7 minutes, then drain in a colander (discarding the liquid).

Pack the artichokes into sterilised jars with extra garlic cloves, bay leaves and oregano, and cover with oil. Leave for approximately 2 months before eating.

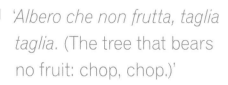

'*Albero che non frutta, taglia taglia.* (The tree that bears no fruit: chop, chop.)'

THE HOME GARDEN

The concept of a garden is very different in the Italian world. No decorative shrubs or flowerbeds and minimal lawn. Here, soil is for vegetables and herbs – fragrant, generous mounds of them – and fruit trees.

You'll find large, soft-leafed basil in old concrete laundry tubs; fennel plants higher than your head; and rosemary in abundance. And depending on what sort of space there is, there'll be pots or rows of tomatoes, zucchini, eggplants, capsicums, garlic and chillies. When Italians buy houses, they transform existing gardens into little farms.

Surrounding the productive areas of a backyard, there is usually plenty of concrete for ease of maintenance – making it so much easier to keep all that vegetation under control. The roar of the lawnmower isn't to be heard from an Italian residence. Guy Grossi remembers his father casting a critical eye over their family garden: 'If a plant didn't bear fruit, then it would be replaced with concrete slabs – there was nothing in between for my father!'

'His garden was full of beautiful fruit trees like apricots and peaches, apples and pears. He also used to grow prickly pears; we used to always get prickles in our fingers peeling them. The resilient herbs like rosemary and sage were in the front garden, and the seasonal herbs like basil and parsley were always grown too. Then there were the vegetables: zucchini, pumpkins, eggplants, beans. It was all beautiful produce and you could just go out and pick some and then that was what was for dinner.'

As Patrizia Simone explains, 'Nobody has it in mind to go to the shops to buy herbs – it's not the way we think. In Italy, even in little apartments, people have their terracotta pots with basil and parsley at the very least. It's all about good flavours and something that anchors you to the land. It brings you back to nature.'

Armando Percuoco was in raptures when he discovered that the traces of iron in the bore water on his country estate made for exceptional parsley. 'Growing things like that is a creative outlet and it gives so much pleasure,' he says.

Part of the joy of gardening is knowing that it is where you've put down roots. The other joy is that you're self-reliant – and you know what you've grown has no additives or pesticides to interfere with the flavour and goodness of your produce.

'My grandmother grew potatoes and would always know how they would perform for her gnocchi,' explains Stefano Manfredi. 'If you buy them from the shops, you can have potatoes that will work one day and a couple of weeks later they will be completely different as they're grown in very different places.'

Rosa Mitchell says her family's pantry *was* the garden. 'You'd never know what you'd have for dinner – whatever was ripe was picked for dinner that afternoon … Pick it fresh. Just as much as you need.'

FRITELLI DI FIORE DI ZUCCHINI

ZUCCHINI FLOWER FRITTERS

FROM LINA SICILIANO

15 zucchini flowers removed
   from their stems
2 heaped tablespoons
   plain flour
2 heaped tablespoons
   self-raising flour
1 tablespoon cornflour
approximately 250 ml
   lukewarm water
salt and pepper
3 large parsley sprigs,
   finely chopped
80 ml extra-virgin olive oil

This is a great recipe to cook if you grow zucchini at home. The flowers are removed from their stems and sliced, so you can use male flowers, which are the ones attached to long, thin stems. (Save the female flowers, attached to baby zucchini, for stuffing.)

Remove the stamens from the male zucchini flowers, and the pistils from the female flowers. Rinse the flowers in cold water and set aside to drain.

Mix the flours in a bowl. Add the water to make a paste of medium consistency (not too runny or too thick) and season with salt and pepper. Stir in the parsley.

Squeeze excess water from the flowers and slice them 1 cm thick. Stir into the flour mixture.

Heat the oil in a frying pan and add heaped tablespoons of mixture, flattening to about 1 cm thick. Fry until golden brown on each side. Drain on paper towel and continue cooking fritters until you have used up the mixture. (Add more oil if necessary.) Serve hot.

Serves 2

'The flowers of tomorrow are
from the seeds of today.'

MINESTRONE

FROM STEFANO MANFREDI

3 tablespoons extra-virgin
    olive oil
2 onions, diced
8 garlic cloves, each cut
    into 3–4 pieces
1 celery heart including the
    pale, tender leaves, sliced
2 large or 4–5 smaller carrots,
    cut into bite-sized pieces
2 cups roughly chopped savoy
    cabbage
2 bay leaves
1 cup fresh flageolet beans,
    or other fresh (or cooked
    dried) beans
350 g waxy potatoes such as
    desiree, peeled and diced
200 g tinned Italian tomatoes,
    crushed
100 g carnaroli rice
salt
150 g spinach, roughly
    chopped
1 cup flat-leaf parsley leaves,
    roughly chopped
60 g parmesan rind, cut into
    1 cm cubes
freshly ground black pepper
freshly grated parmesan
    to serve

This fabulous touch-your-heart soup full of fresh vegetables was eaten at least once a week as Stefano was growing up. The use of parmesan rind to deepen the flavour is very clever.

Minestrone is a soup that gets better with age, so while it's good the day you make it, it's even better the day after.

Heat the oil in a heavy-based pot and add the onion, garlic, celery heart, carrot, cabbage and bay leaves. Lightly fry the vegetables for 2–3 minutes without letting them colour. Stir in the beans, potato and tomato, then cover the ingredients with water. Once the soup comes to the boil, add the rice and turn down to a simmer. Add a few good pinches of salt and simmer for 20–25 minutes.

Add the spinach, parsley and parmesan rind and simmer for another 5 minutes. Remove from the heat and taste for seasoning, adding extra salt if needed, and pepper. Serve with plenty of grated parmesan and crusty bread.

Serves 10

'It's important to remember that every Italian meal is a celebration, no matter how simple the food.'

ORECCHIETTE CON CIME DI RAPA

ORECCHIETTE WITH BROCCOLI RABE

FROM GUY GROSSI

500 g dried orecchiette
1 bunch broccoli rabe,
    roughly chopped
3 tablespoons olive oil
1 garlic clove, finely sliced
1 small red chilli, chopped
50 g pancetta, cut into batons
a few basil leaves, crushed to a
    paste with 1 teaspoon olive
    oil
sea salt
freshly ground black pepper
1 heaped tablespoon finely
    chopped flat-leaf parsley
grated pecorino

Broccoli rabe, or rapini, is a bitter green that comes into season in autumn. It is a member of the turnip family and you will find it at selected greengrocers in bundles of large leaves with broccoli-like flower heads opening into small yellow flowers.

Guy learnt this dish from his father, Pietro, who is from Puglia in southern Italy. It's earthy and rustic – a peasant-style dish to get you through the day.

Bring a large pot of salted water to the boil and add the orecchiette and broccoli rabe. Cook until the orecchiette is al dente.

Meanwhile, heat the olive oil in a large frying pan and add the garlic, chilli and pancetta. Fry over medium heat for 1 minute, then add the basil oil and season with salt and pepper.

Add the drained orecchiette and broccoli rabe to the pan and toss to coat in the oil. Add the parsley and grated pecorino to taste. Toss briefly, then remove from the heat and serve.

Serves 6

'"*Cammina chi pantofole fino a quando non hai i scarpe*" (Walk with your slippers until you find your shoes) means do your best with what you have until things improve.)'

PATATE, PEPE E MELANZANE FRITTI
FRIED POTATO, CAPSICUM AND EGGPLANT
(A TRADITIONAL FARMER'S LUNCH)

FROM LINA SICILIANO

185 ml extra-virgin olive oil
2 medium potatoes, peeled
and cut into 5 mm wedges
1 small eggplant
2 medium red capsicums
(preferably *corno di toro*
– bull's horn), cut into
2 cm strips
2 garlic cloves, chopped
1 medium tomato, thinly sliced
6 basil leaves
salt

Lina serves this with crusty homemade bread, and says the vegetables are also good cold in a bread roll.

Heat the oil in a large frying pan and add the potatoes. Fry until lightly golden, then remove from the oil and place on a warm plate. Keep warm.

Peel and finely slice the eggplant (it is best to do this just before cooking so it doesn't go brown) and add to the pan along with the capsicum. Stir-fry until just soft, then return the potatoes to the pan and stir everything together.

Move the ingredients to the edges of the pan to create a gap in the middle. Add the garlic to the gap and fry for 5 seconds until it releases its aroma, then add the tomato, basil and salt to taste and stir for 10 seconds. Serve with crusty bread.

Serves 2

'An Italian meal is
never without bread.'

'Your most faithful friends are your own hands.'

CARCIOFI ALLA ROMANA
STUFFED ARTICHOKES

FROM GUY GROSSI

1 lemon, zested and juiced
12 artichokes
½ cup chopped flat-leaf parsley
2 tablespoons chopped sage
2 tablespoons chopped mint
1 garlic clove, finely chopped
½ teaspoon chopped red chilli
1 cup freshly grated parmigiano reggiano
3 cups dried breadcrumbs
300 ml extra-virgin olive oil, plus extra for drizzling
250 ml white wine
sea salt
freshly ground black pepper

The Romans have been cooking and eating artichokes for centuries. Guy's father taught him to stuff artichokes this way; he gathered all the family around and they prepared them together.

Fill a large bowl with cold water and add the lemon juice. Take an artichoke and peel off the outer leaves until you reach the paler inner leaves. Cut off the stem and slice off the top of the artichoke so the heart is visible, and scoop out the hairy choke. Put the trimmed artichoke into the bowl of water to prevent discolouration and continue preparing the remaining artichokes.

Combine the lemon zest, herbs, garlic, chilli, parmigiano reggiano, bread-crumbs and oil in a bowl. Season with salt and pepper and mix well.

Preheat the oven to 180°C. Drain the artichokes, then stuff each one generously with the breadcrumb mixture by gently separating each leaf and pushing the stuffing into the gaps. Tightly pack the artichokes into a baking dish and drizzle with more oil. Pour in the white wine and add water to just cover the artichokes. Season with more salt and pepper. Cover with foil and bake in the oven for about 20 minutes, or until the artichokes are tender when pierced with a skewer.

Serves 6

'La verdura è una pietanza che vuol olio in abbondanza. (A vegetable dish means oil in abundance).'

INSALATA DI FINOCCHIO

FENNEL SALAD

FROM GUY GROSSI

2 fennel bulbs
2 juicy oranges
½ red onion, finely sliced
2 heads of radicchio, cores cut
    out, sliced 2–3 cm thick
3 tablespoons extra-virgin
    olive oil
1½ tablespoons white-wine
    vinegar
sea salt
freshly ground black pepper
½ cup flat-leaf parsley leaves

This glorious winter salad is full of fresh, clean flavours and goes with any fish dish, or can be eaten on its own. Make sure you slice the fennel as finely as possible (a mandolin is a great help).

Cut the tops off the fennel bulbs and discard. Cut the bulbs in half through the core and slice very finely. Place in a large bowl.

Use a small, sharp knife to cut the peel from the oranges, making sure to remove all the white pith. Hold the oranges over a bowl to catch any juice and cut on either side of each segment to remove wedges of flesh, leaving the membranes behind. Add the segments to the fennel. Squeeze the juice from the membranes and set the bowl of juice aside for the dressing.

Add the onion and radicchio to the fennel and orange.

Whisk the oil and vinegar into the orange juice and pour over the salad. Season with salt and pepper and toss together. Check the seasoning, then add the parsley leaves and briefly toss again.

Serves 8

'A salad requires four people to make it properly – a miser to put in the wine vinegar, a spendthrift to add the olive oil, a sensible person to add the salt and a crazy one to mix it.'

BREAD AND PIZZA

It's the weak-at-the-knees smell that hits you when the heavy iron door is removed from the big clay and brick oven – it makes you swoon and salivate. Freshly baked bread, toasty and golden and yeasty and warm, with an aroma so powerful you can almost *see* it … now this is bread!

Such is the dedication to this bread that many Italians who settled in Australia constructed their own wood-fired ovens. That way they could continue the traditions of the village – the heavy, crusty *pane di casa* loaves that are delicious simply dipped into olive oil or served with antipasto, or a few days later toasted up as bruschetta, or cubed and popped into the oven for the bread salad called *panzanella* that is a sponge for good olive oil, balsamic vinegar and sweet tomatoes.

Guy Grossi remembers his mother's rule: 'If you drop your bread on the ground, pick it up and kiss it immediately because the bread comes from God.' Respect for the most basic of food is drummed in and never forgotten.

Guy recalls a memorable visit to a Chinese restaurant with his father when he was a boy. 'Dad took us to our first-ever Chinese restaurant and he was shocked. He said, "How can you have a restaurant with no bread?"'

'Never, ever, waste bread – it is a sin,' Rosa Matto recalls her mother saying. 'That's why we have so, so many recipes that use up stale bread. For religious people, it represents the body of Christ, and for poor, rural people it was just unthinkable to waste a staple food.'

For artisan baker Daniel Chirico, making bread is an incredibly creative and beautiful process: 'There is a real interaction nurturing something from its raw state … It's working with a living organism – you watch it grow and you work with it.'

'Mum would bake bread on a weekly basis,' remembers Daniel. 'She'd make a big batch of dough to make pizzas for us and because she was making the dough that day, she would make a couple of loaves of bread too.'

'It's a matter of pride that recipes are passed on from generation to generation,' says Guy Grossi. 'Recipes are very much the same in every region, like tomato sauce, but you find that every family has a slightly different way of preparing it. One family will cook the onions, one will add a tiny bit of chilli. Each family does something that others don't. Passing on traditions in the family is like a father teaching his son how to hunt or fish.

'My father taught me his way to sear meat so it retains the best flavour and my mum showed me her secret to making gnocchi – why you can't measure flour when you're making it [instead you need to watch for the texture]. Every time I make gnocchi I think of my mum because it's her recipe and her gnocchi is my benchmark. It's embracing your family history through the recipes. It comes from something that's very close to your heart.'

Italian bread has a light crumb and is not overly flavoured, so it's a perfect vehicle for sauces. And then there's the crust – ideally so crusty you can *hear* it when you tear the bread apart.

'Bread is essential with pasta. You have your fork in your right hand and bread in the left and as you get closer to the bottom of the bowl, the left hand starts working harder as the bread catches all that great sauce. It's a classic image of an Italian!' Daniel Chirico

CORN AND RICOTTA
PAGNOTTA

FROM DANIEL CHIRICO

1 kg unbleached strong flour,
   plus extra for dusting
440 g maize (corn) flour
300 g fresh ricotta
35 g sea salt
10 g honey
35 g fresh yeast
   (or 1 tablespoon (15 g)
   dried yeast if unavailable)
1 litre water at room
   temperature
semolina for dusting

A good trick that Daniel's nonna taught him was to half-fill a kitchen sink with hot water and place bread dough in the cupboard underneath to prove. It creates a warm, draught-free environment for the dough to rise.

For the best results in this recipe, use organic flour, organic forest honey, fresh yeast and filtered water, as Daniel does.

Put the flours, ricotta, salt and honey in a large bowl. Add the yeast to the water and stir to dissolve, then add to the flour mixture. Combine with your hands to form a dough. Transfer to a work surface and knead for at least 10 minutes. Return the dough to the bowl and cover with plastic wrap. Leave to prove in a warm, draught-free place for approximately 2 hours, until doubled in size.

Turn the dough out onto a floured surface and divide into 3 or 4 pieces, to make 3 larger or 4 smaller loaves. Shape into balls. Cover with a tea towel and leave to rest for 30 minutes away from any draughts.

Line some medium-sized bowls (around 20 cm wide) with tea towels and dust the towels with flour. Firmly reshape the balls of dough and place seam-side up in the bowls. Leave to prove in a warm, draught-free place for 1–2 hours, until doubled in size.

Preheat the oven to 220°C. Lightly dust some trays with semolina. Gently turn the loaves onto the trays and bake for 30–40 minutes, until golden.

Makes 3–4 loaves

'Il pane apre tutte le bocche.
(Bread opens all mouths.)'

HAZELNUT AND FIG BREAD

FROM DANIEL CHIRICO

800 g unbleached strong
   flour, plus extra for dusting
200 g spelt flour
22 g sea salt
30 g fresh yeast
   (or 1 tablespoon (15 g) dried
   yeast if unavailable)
800 ml water at room
   temperature
400 g hazelnuts, roasted and
   skinned
300 g dried figs, diced

Daniel uses only organic flours, fresh yeast and filtered water in his artisan breads.

Put the flours and salt into a large bowl. Add the yeast to the water and stir to dissolve, then add to the flour mixture. Combine with your hands to form a dough, adding a little more water if necessary. Transfer to a work surface and knead for at least 10 minutes.

Return the dough to the bowl and knead in the hazelnuts and figs until well combined. Cover with plastic wrap and leave to prove in a warm, draught-free place for approximately 2 hours, until doubled in size.

Turn the dough out onto a floured surface and divide into 4 even pieces. Shape into balls. Cover with a tea towel and leave to rest for 30 minutes away from any draughts.

Brush or spray oil inside 4 small bread tins. Lengthen the balls to fit into the tins and place inside the tins seam-side down. Leave to prove in a warm, draught-free place for 1–2 hours, until doubled in size.

Preheat the oven to 220°C. Lightly sprinkle flour over the tops of the loaves and place in the oven. Bake for 30–40 minutes, until golden. Remove the loaves from the tins and set on a wire rack to cool.

Makes 4 small loaves

'We can't eat unless God is at the table,'
referring to the bread.

A phrase Daniela Mollica remembers her grandparents saying

BRUSCHETTA

FROM GUY GROSSI

MUSHROOM TOPPING
olive oil
frozen porcini (cepe)
  mushrooms, thawed
  and sliced

CHERRY TOMATO TOPPING
olive oil
1 onion, finely chopped
2 handfuls cherry tomatoes
basil leaves

thickly sliced ciabatta
1 garlic clove, cut in half
handful of flat-leaf parsley
  leaves, finely shredded
extra-virgin olive oil
sea salt
freshly ground black pepper

Bruschetta is so simple and shows that food doesn't have to be fancy to be extremely tasty and satisfying. But you do have to start with good ingredients – the bread to begin with, and the toppings. Tomatoes must be ripe and sweet, and I like to use imported porcini mushrooms (available frozen at good delis), but you can use other local wild mushrooms if you prefer.

For the mushroom topping, heat some oil in a frying pan and sauté the mushrooms until golden.

For the cherry tomato topping, heat some oil in another pan and gently sauté the onion until caramelised. Add the cherry tomatoes and stir until lightly softened.

Toast the bread in a dry chargrill pan. Rub the cut garlic clove onto one side of each piece of toast and sprinkle with parsley. Drizzle with extra-virgin olive oil and spoon on the mushroom or tomato topping. For the tomato topping, scatter with basil leaves. Season with salt and pepper.

'Troubles are fewer when there is bread on the table.'

PIZZA MARGHERITA

FROM ALESSANDRO D'AURIA

DOUGH
375 ml warm water
20 g fresh yeast
   (or 3 teaspoons (10 g) dried
   yeast if unavailable)
1 teaspoon salt
3 tablespoons olive oil
1 teaspoon sugar
500 g strong flour

TOPPING
1 tablespoon olive oil
2 garlic cloves, crushed
185 ml tomato puree
75 g parmesan, finely grated
400 g mozzarella,
   thinly sliced
1 cup basil leaves
salt
freshly ground black pepper

Alessandro makes his pizza dough by feel and sight, so these quantities are just a guide and you may need to add a little more flour or water.

To make the dough, pour the warm water into a large bowl and add the yeast, stirring until dissolved. Stir in the salt, oil and sugar, then add the flour and mix with your hands to form a dough. If it seems too wet or too dry, you may need to add a little more flour or water. Transfer to a work surface and knead until silky smooth and elastic (around 10 minutes). Return the dough to the bowl and cover with plastic wrap. Place a heavy cloth on top and set aside in a warm place until the dough doubles in size (this usually takes around 2½ hours).

Oil 2 large oven trays (Alessandro uses rectangular trays 28 × 35 cm in dimension). Take the risen dough out of the bowl and divide it in half. Form each piece into a rectangle (or circle if using round trays) and stretch the dough with your hands to cover the trays. The dough will have some resistance, but will eventually settle.

Preheat the oven to 200°C. To prepare the topping, mix the oil with the garlic and brush over the pizzas. Spread the tomato puree over the top, leaving a border around the edges of the pizzas to form the *cornichone* (crust). Set aside in a warm place for another 30 minutes to allow the crusts to puff slightly. Sprinkle the pizzas with the parmesan and top with the mozzarella. Dot with the basil leaves and season with salt and pepper. Bake in the oven until the bottoms of the pizzas are golden brown and the edges have risen (up to 25 minutes). Slice and serve immediately.

Serves 4–6

"'*Mangia!* (Eat!)" was part of my mother's personal dialect. It meant, "I love you," and, "My food is the way I nourish you – physically, spiritually, morally." Underlining the words was a delicate warning: "Refuse my food? *Guaio!*"' Rosa Matto

PIZZA

One of Italy's great gifts to the world is pizza, which was created – so the story goes – in Naples when some dough was flattened, shaped into a circle and baked with a smear of tomato sauce on top. This was the original marinara pizza, made for the mariners and having nothing to do with seafood toppings.

More toppings were added as the years went by – the classic colours of the Italian flag were created for Queen Margherita with the additions of mozzarella and basil. The Italians value the simplicity of a few high-quality ingredients.

To make pizza bases, the general rule is that the longer it takes to make the dough, the nicer it is, says Guy Grossi. 'Let the dough take time to prove. The base should be thin and have a bit of crunch to it, but it shouldn't be like a biscuit – it needs some body as well. But there is nothing worse than a pizza base that is thick and like a cake!'

When you're shaping the dough into a pizza, you should form a small raised rim around the pizza called the *'cornichone'*. It is the crunchiest part of the pizza and holds in the topping.

How the pizza is cooked is also crucial. Guy says the best pizzas are baked in ovens with stone floors. 'Whether that needs to be a wood-fired oven or a gas oven is a matter of opinion,' he says. 'Some people argue that the only way to cook great pizza is in a wood-fired oven, but others say no, no, no, you can still do it in a gas-fired oven. Both can be equally as good as long as the pizza cooks at the right temperature – the oven needs to very, very hot. Then the base of the pizza crisps and you get that little bit of rise in the dough, or what we call in Italian, *"un salto"* – a little jump!'

GRISSINI

FROM GUY GROSSI

25 g fresh yeast
    (or 3 teaspoons (12 g)
    dried yeast if unavailable)
320 ml warm water
1 teaspoon liquid malt extract
3 tablespoons extra-virgin
    olive oil
1 tablespoon lard, softened
625 g plain flour
sea salt

Making grissini shows you've gone to real effort to make a special meal, and they are perfect served with antipasto.

The bread sticks are very delicate and need to be handled with care. The trick is to let the dough prove slowly, and when it has doubled in size, to cut and stretch it into sticks by hand. If the dough is left too long, the grissini can break when you're trying to make them.

Put the yeast and warm water in a bowl and stir until the yeast dissolves. Add the remaining ingredients, including a pinch of salt, and use your hands to mix into a dough. Transfer to a work surface and knead for 10–15 minutes, until smooth, shiny and elastic. (The dough can also be made in an electric mixer with a dough hook.) Roll the dough into a log 10 cm wide, cover with a damp tea towel and leave in a warm spot until doubled in size.

Preheat the oven to 170°C. Slice the log into strips 2 cm wide and use your fingers to pull the strips into long sticks. Place on trays and sprinkle with salt. Bake for 15–20 minutes, until lightly coloured and dry. The grissini can be stored in an airtight container for up to 1 week.

Makes approximately 25 grissini

'My mother still makes the sign of the cross over the dough before she puts the bread in the oven. And I always say a silent prayer when I'm baking too.' Rosa Matto

PANZANELLA
BREAD SALAD

FROM GUY GROSSI

15 cm of stale sourdough
  baguette, cut into bite-sized
  chunks
3 vine-ripened tomatoes,
  diced
½ red onion, finely sliced
handful of basil leaves
handful of flat-leaf parsley
  leaves, shredded
sea salt
freshly ground black pepper
2½ tablespoons extra-virgin
  olive oil
1½ tablespoons aged
  balsamic vinegar

Panzanella is a great example of Italians not wasting anything. It's a traditional Tuscan salad made with toasted stale bread, bursting with the freshness of tomato and basil.

Toast the bread in a 180°C oven until dry and lightly coloured. Leave to cool.

Combine the bread, tomato and onion in a bowl. Tear over the basil leaves and add the parsley. Season with salt and pepper. Drizzle with the oil and vinegar and toss thoroughly before serving.

Serves 2

'*Meglio un uovo oggi che una gallina domani.* (Better an egg today then a hen tomorrow, meaning take every opportunity as it comes along.)'

ROASTED CAPSICUMS

capsicums
olive oil
sea salt

Roasted capsicums can be used in many recipes. Toss them with olive oil and balsamic vinegar to serve as an antipasto, or lightly pan-fry them in oil and garlic to serve on polenta. Choose any colour capsicum you like, or use a variety of colours.

Preheat the oven to 210°C. Place the capsicums on a tray and liberally douse with oil, massaging into every crevice. Season with salt. Roast the capsicums in the oven for 15 minutes. Turn the capsicums and continue roasting and turning every so often until all sides have come into contact with the tray and the capsicums are blackened and soft.

Place the hot capsicums in a plastic or paper bag and allow to cool – the steam will help loosen the skins. When cool enough to handle, pull out the stems and tear the capsicums in half. Remove the seeds and skins.

'When my mother is cooking no one is allowed anywhere near the kitchen, she says "*Levati da mezzo i piedi*", which means get out from under my feet!'

TARALLI NAPOLETANI

FROM LUCIANA SAMPOGNA

15 g fresh yeast
   (or 2 teaspoons (7 g)
   dried yeast if unavailable)
200 ml warm water
500 g plain flour
15 g salt
3 teaspoons freshly
   ground black pepper
150 g lard, softened
200 g raw almonds, chopped

Stir the yeast into the water until dissolved. Put the flour, salt, pepper and lard in a bowl and mix in the water and yeast with your hands. If the dough seems dry, add a little more water (try another tablespoon or so). Transfer to a work surface and knead for 6 minutes. Knead in the almonds at the end. Return the dough to the bowl, cover with a tea towel and let it rise for 30 minutes (it should puff a little).

Lightly grease some trays with extra lard, and preheat the oven to 200°C. Roll the dough into a sausage about 2.5 cm thick. Flatten it with the tips of your fingers and cut it into sticks about 1 cm wide. Roll each stick smooth, then bend the stick and cross over the ends, creating a loop. Arrange on the trays. Bake in the oven for 15 minutes.

When all the biscuits are baked, transfer them to one tray. Reduce the oven temperature to 160°C and bake the biscuits for another 10–15 minutes. Then, reduce the temperature to 130°C and bake for another 20–30 minutes. The biscuits should be golden brown and crisp. When cool, store in an airtight container.

Makes 25 biscuits

THE WILD HARVEST

The soft early-morning light slanting through the pine trees, the smell of pine needles and rich earth, and the muffled sounds … this is the secret world of mushroom gathering. For many Italian families, particularly those from the mountainous regions of Italy, the mushroom hunt is an all-hands-on-deck event.

Early on, children in Italy are taught what's edible and not; how to spot the prized orange pine mushrooms, slippery jacks and porcinis. Adelina Pulford remembers getting up at 4 am to search the local forests and later trooping back through the village with baskets of fragrant porcini mushrooms.

'The smell of porcini is quite strong and unmistakable. They smell like the bush and the trees you are surrounded by at the time; it is a rich and earthy smell,' says Adelina.

For a young Angelo Bonacci, autumn days in Italy would begin with the call, '*Paesano! Amico! Andiamo a funghi che tempo e venuto perche e autunno e piogguto!*' Angelo is now considered the King of Mushrooms in his new Australian home and he makes that call himself. It means 'Friends! The time is right, the autumn rains are here so let's go mushroom hunting!'

Italians love to sauté their mushrooms with garlic, parsley and onion and toss them with spaghetti, or bake them with potatoes, olive oil, garlic and sage, or turn them into a frittata. Some mushrooms are laid out to be dried; others are peeled, sliced and preserved; and others are preserved whole.

Aron Michielli recalls his large front garden in Italy covered in old white sheets. 'These would be covered in thinly sliced mushrooms at the beginning of the season when it was still warm and sunny to dry them. The freezer in the cellar basement was full of mixed mushroom *trifolati* [sautéed mushrooms] and all the shelving there was filled with pickled mushrooms and tomato passata.'

From mushrooms to fennel, gathering food from the wild is not only fun, but results in flavours that are simply not available in shops. Patrizia Simone prefers wild fennel for flavouring sausages and salami because it is beautifully mild. 'It works with the other flavours better than what you'd buy. You can also use it to make a pesto to serve with fish, which is lovely,' she says.

'Never feast on *funghi* at night
or you'll have heavy dreams!'

Rosa Mitchell loves collecting wild fennel, mushrooms and cardoons (a thistle-like plant with edible stalks), and using the produce in her restaurant. 'Often I'm driving along with my husband and I get him to go back when I see things growing by the side of the road.'

Rosa Matto recalls family picnics when she was a child. 'My mother and the aunties went off gathering weeds – to our great humiliation. But when they returned with nettles, wild rocket, nasturtium leaves and horse chestnuts, we were always the first to line up for the delicious, bitter salad.'

Hunting, of course, is also part of the wild harvest, especially during winter – for everything from quail and rabbit to wild boar. This is a tradition that originally came from necessity in Italy, explains Guy Grossi. 'Then it became a cultural thing … There are many Italians who love to hunt and forage for wild foods,' he says.

One of them is Daniel Airo-Farulla, who learnt how to hunt from his grandfather when he was five or six years old – a young boy donning earmuffs. 'I learnt you don't say a word when you go hunting – it's the cone of silence and you learn not to close the car doors!'

PAPPARDELLE CON FUNGHI DI BOSCO

PAPPARDELLE WITH FOREST MUSHROOMS

FROM ARON MICHIELLI

200 g fresh pappardelle
(page 125 and 134)
splash of extra-virgin olive oil
1 garlic clove, finely sliced
1 teaspoon chopped sage,
marjoram or thyme leaves
2 medium slippery jack
mushrooms, sponge
removed and roughly sliced
2 medium pine mushrooms,
roughly sliced
150 ml white wine
salt and pepper
1 tablespoon butter
1 tablespoon chopped
flat-leaf parsley
freshly grated parmigiano
reggiano

Put a pot of salted water on to boil for the pasta. While you wait, heat the oil in a large frying pan and sauté the garlic with the sage, marjoram or thyme. Add the mushrooms and sauté for another 2–3 minutes.

Meanwhile, add the pappardelle to the boiling water and cook until al dente (fresh pasta should not take more than 3 or 4 minutes).

Add the wine to the mushrooms and let it reduce for 1 minute. Season with salt and pepper. When the pasta is ready, drain it, reserving some cooking water, and stir into the mushroom sauce, heating together briefly. Add the butter and a little of the cooking water if the pasta seems dry. Serve sprinkled with parsley and parmigiano reggiano.

Serves 2

'Always keep some pasta water to add to your sauce if it is too dry.'

PASTA CON SALSICCIA E FUNGHI
PASTA WITH SAUSAGE AND MUSHROOM

FROM GUY GROSSI

500 g fresh scialatielli, or
 dried maccheroni or trofie
100 ml olive oil
6 pork and fennel sausages,
 meat squeezed from the
 casings
1 garlic clove, crushed
100 g morel mushrooms
 (or other wild mushrooms),
 well rinsed and roughly sliced
150 g swiss brown mushrooms,
 roughly sliced
150 g oyster mushrooms,
 roughly sliced
2 tablespoons chopped sage
sea salt
freshly ground black pepper
2 tablespoons chopped flat-leaf
 parsley
splash of white wine
100 g parmigiano reggiano,
 grated

For this autumnal dish Guy likes to make fresh scialatielli, which is like a fat tagliatelle. Otherwise, he uses dried short pasta such as maccheroni or trofie.

Cook the pasta in salted boiling water until al dente. While the pasta is cooking, heat the olive oil in a frying pan over medium heat. Add the sausage meat in spoonfuls, then add the garlic. Brown the meat, stirring to break it up. Add the mushrooms and continue to stir. Add the sage, season carefully with salt and pepper and cook for another few minutes until the mushrooms are tender. Add the parsley and wine.

Drain the pasta and add to the mushrooms, tossing to combine. Remove from the heat and stir through the parmigiano reggiano.

Serves 6

'Hunger is the best sauce.'

'You long for mushroom time, that wonderful season. It's all about the flavour – the results are delicious.' Patrizia Simone

TORTELLINI DI ANATRA E PORCINI CON PERA CARAMELATA

DUCK AND PORCINI TORTELLINI WITH CARAMELISED PEAR

FROM GUY GROSSI

ROASTED DUCK
2.2 kg duck
sprig of rosemary
sprig of sage
1 teaspoon juniper berries, crushed
1 star anise, crushed
sea salt
freshly ground black pepper
125 ml olive oil

TORTELLINI
meat from the roasted duck
olive oil
1 onion, chopped
1 garlic clove, sliced
1 celery stalk, sliced
100 g ciabatta, roughly chopped, briefly soaked in water and squeezed dry
sea salt
freshly ground black pepper
2 tablespoons tomato paste
100 ml marsala
2½ tablespoons white wine
100 g frozen porcini (cepe) mushrooms, thawed and sliced
¼ cup freshly grated parmigiano reggiano
300 g fresh pasta sheets (page 125)

PEAR
1 large, firm pear, cored and cut into 1 cm cubes
100 g (½ cup) brown sugar
200 ml white wine

knob of butter

The duck for the tortellini is roasted first – the idea is that when you put a little parcel in your mouth, you think of roasted duck with hints of mushrooms.

Preheat the oven to 180°C. Put the rosemary and sage into the cavity of the duck. Place the duck on a tray and sprinkle with the crushed juniper berries, star anise and some salt and pepper, rubbing the mixture into the skin. Drizzle with the olive oil and roast for approximately 40–45 minutes, until cooked through. Allow to cool slightly, then take the meat from the bones.

To make the filling for the tortellini, roughly chop the duck meat including the skin. Heat 2½ tablespoons of olive oil in a heavy-based saucepan and sauté the onion, garlic and celery until softened. Add the moistened bread and duck meat and season with salt and pepper. Add the tomato paste, marsala and wine and cook for a few minutes, then remove from the heat.

Briefly sauté the mushrooms in a frying pan and add to the duck mixture. Allow the mixture to cool before mincing or chopping it coarsely. Add the parmigiano reggiano and mix well.

Cut the pasta sheets into approximately 60 circles, 7–8 cm in diameter. Put a small amount of filling in the centre of each circle. To make a tortellini, lightly moisten the edge of a circle with water. Fold the circle in half and lightly press the edges to seal. Fold the rim of the tortellini down and bring the two corners around to meet, pressing together to seal. Continue making the tortellini, then set aside on a lightly floured work surface while you cook the pear.

Put the pear, brown sugar and wine in a frying pan over medium heat and cook slowly for around 10 minutes, until the pear is soft and the sugar begins to caramelise.

Bring a pot of salted water to the boil and cook the tortellini for 4–5 minutes. Drain and toss with the caramelised pear and the knob of butter.

Serves 6

QUAIL, PORCINI AND CHESTNUT INVOLTINI

FROM DANNY RUSSO

QUAIL INVOLTINI
8 quail
½ cup dried porcini
    mushrooms, softened in
    water and roughly chopped
8 chestnuts, boiled, peeled
    and chopped
400 g minced chicken
2 thyme sprigs, leaves picked
40 g parmesan, grated
grated zest of 1 lemon
40 g fresh breadcrumbs
salt and pepper

QUAIL STOCK
bones from the quail
½ onion, diced
1 small carrot, diced
1 small celery stalk, diced
100 ml madeira
2 garlic cloves, peeled
sprig of thyme
sprig of rosemary
1 bay leaf
1 tomato, roughly chopped
2 litres water

PORCINI SALT
40 g sea salt
10 g dried porcini mushrooms

TO FINISH
extra-virgin olive oil
4 frozen porcini (cepe)
    mushrooms, thawed
    and cut into quarters
1 tablespoon chopped
    flat-leaf parsley

This a delicious Calabrese dish from top chef Danny Russo. Make it and fall in love.

To bone the quail for the involtini, find the wishbone at the top of the breast by pushing back the skin and use a small, sharp knife to cut it out. (Reserve all bones for the stock.) Cut on either side of the backbone with a pair of kitchen scissors to remove the backbone, and open the bird up. Detach the ribs with the tip of the knife and pull them out. Carefully cut out the breastbone. Check the quail for any remaining bones (the leg and wing bones should remain intact).

Place the remaining ingredients for the involtini (the stuffing) in a bowl, seasoning with salt and pepper. Mix thoroughly and set aside to allow the flavours to develop.

To make the quail stock, preheat the oven to 180°C. Put the quail bones, onion, carrot and celery on a tray and roast for around 30 minutes, until golden brown. Remove from the oven and deglaze the tray with the madeira, scraping any roasted meat and vegetables from the bottom. Tip the contents of the tray into a saucepan, add the remaining ingredients and simmer for 1½ hours.

To make the porcini salt, crush the salt and dried mushrooms in a mortar until fine.

To assemble the quail involtini, lay the boned quail skin-side down on a board and season well. Place some stuffing in the middle of each bird, then roll up into a neat parcel. Tie with butcher's string to hold the bird and stuffing in place.

To finish, preheat the oven to 180°C. Heat some oil in a frying pan over medium heat and lightly brown the quail all over. Transfer to a tray and roast in the oven for 10–15 minutes.

Sauté the quartered porcini mushrooms in the frying pan with another splash of oil. Deglaze the pan with ½ cup of strained quail stock, and add the parsley. Place the mushrooms on plates and sit the roasted quail on top. Sprinkle with the porcini salt and drizzle with more oil.

Serves 8

SICILIAN SWEET
AND SOUR RABBIT

FROM DANIEL AIRO-FARULLA AND GUY GROSSI

MARINATED RABBIT

2 rabbits

2 litres water

juice of 1 lemon

5 thyme sprigs, leaves picked
and roughly chopped

2 rosemary sprigs, leaves
picked and roughly
chopped

6 bay leaves

10 sage leaves

¼ cup chopped flat-leaf
parsley

2 small red chillies, finely
chopped

100 ml olive oil

sea salt

freshly ground black pepper

80 ml olive oil for frying

1 large onion, chopped

1 large leek, chopped

2 garlic cloves, finely chopped

2 carrots, chopped

2 celery stalks, chopped

12 shallots, peeled

6 kipfler potatoes, halved

250 ml chicken stock

100 ml white wine

2½ tablespoons chardonnay
vinegar

2 tablespoons pine nuts

2 tablespoons sultanas

2 tablespoons sugar

Soak the rabbits in the water and lemon juice for 1 hour (this helps to tenderise the meat). Cut the rabbits into small pieces through the bones. Put into a large mixing bowl with the herbs, chilli and oil. Season with salt and pepper and mix well.

Heat half the oil in a large frying pan and fry the rabbit pieces until golden. Return the rabbit to the bowl of marinade.

Preheat the oven to 180°C. Heat the remaining oil in an ovenproof pot and fry the onion, leek and garlic until golden. Add the carrot and celery and stir for a few minutes, then add the shallots and potatoes and cook for another few minutes. Add the rabbit and marinade, followed by the remaining ingredients. Cover with a lid and bake in the oven for 1–1½ hours.

Serves 6

'"*Non si po avere la carne senza ossa*"
(you can't have meat without the bone)
means you can't have the good things
in life without some of the bad.'

FUNGHI CON PISELLI E RICOTTA SALATA

MUSHROOMS WITH PEAS AND SALTED RICOTTA

FROM EUGENIO MAIALE

extra-virgin olive oil
½ onion, finely chopped
3 teaspoons finely sliced garlic
1 long red chilli, finely sliced
8 medium–large swiss brown
    mushrooms (or a mixture
    of swiss brown and
    portobello), sliced into
    quarters
salt and pepper
150 g freshly shelled peas
2½ tablespoons white wine
8 mint leaves
1½ tablespoons butter
1 teaspoon grated lemon zest
100 g salted ricotta (*ricotta
    salata*), grated

Heat a little oil in a frying pan over high heat and add the onion, garlic and chilli. Fry briefly until the onion begins to soften, then lower the heat and add the mushrooms. Sauté for 5 minutes until lightly golden. Season with salt and pepper.

Add the peas and stir for a couple of minutes, then add the wine and cook over high heat until reduced by half. Tear over the mint leaves, then remove from the heat.

Add the butter and lemon zest and toss until the butter and wine emulsify into a sauce. Spoon onto plates topped with the salted ricotta.

Serves 4

'My mother went to put salt in the water for wild cardoons and my aunty said "No! If you put salt in now, the cardoons go hard."' Rosa Mitchell

TAGLIERINI
CON PORCINI

TAGLIERINI WITH PORCINI MUSHROOMS

FROM GUY GROSSI

100 ml extra-virgin olive oil, plus extra for drizzling
200 g frozen porcini (cepe) mushrooms, thawed and roughly sliced
2 garlic cloves, finely chopped
sea salt
freshly ground black pepper
500 g fresh taglierini
2 tablespoons chopped flat-leaf parsley

Taglierini pasta is a thinner version of tagliatelle.

Bring a pot of salted water to the boil for the pasta.

Meanwhile, heat the oil in a frying pan over medium heat and sauté the mushrooms briefly. Add the garlic, salt and pepper and continue to sauté for a few minutes.

Add the pasta to the boiling water and cook until al dente (about 2 minutes).

Finish the mushroom sauce by adding the parsley and cooking briefly. Drain the pasta and toss through the mushrooms. Drizzle with oil and serve.

Serves 6

'A petra offerto da un amico è come una mela. (A rock offered by a friend is like an apple, meaning you can trust anything from a friend.)'

FISHING

For many Italians, fishing is in the blood. From the little coves of the Mediterranean to the oceans of the world, the techniques are the same – it's 'man amongst the elements' and the sense of satisfaction is immense.

Jim Mendolia is a third-generation fisherman who followed his father Francolino to sea on the Western Australian coast. Francolino came from Sicily and learnt to tell the signs of a good school of fish from his father.

It was while Francolino and his friends fished for lobster that they noticed big schools of their beloved anchovies and sardines, which didn't have a market in Australia at the time. 'People used to be scared of small fish because they didn't know what to do with them – they're used to tasteless, white fillets,' says Jim.

But gradually those tastes have changed. The Mendolias set up a factory to process anchovies and sardines and found a market for their delicious produce. The fishing itself changed too. Jim looks for the same signs his father did – following the birds and dolphins – although he also has a sonar system to locate big schools of fish.

'My type of fishing is really hunting,' he says. 'Even though we've got a big net, we're chasing fish – it's an adrenalin thing – you're chasing, competing with the dolphins – it's the adrenalin pump which is super exciting. It's more immediate, unlike lobsters when you don't get the result until the next day. And I have to say it's also the outdoor thing – working outdoors – it's magic coming home while the sun's coming up.'

Further up the Western Australian coast, crayfisherman Justin Pirrotina is pulling up pots of the delicious sweet crustaceans off the beautiful Abrolhos Islands. He also followed his father into the fishing business and loves the stripped-back simplicity of life on these turquoise atolls. He remembers rowing over to the little schoolhouse as a child, just as his own children now do for a couple of months every year.

The taste of fresh fish is the other great bonus of this lifestyle – the ability to have a barbecue plate entirely covered with crayfish or fish that are no more than an hour out of the water. 'You can't really beat fresh sardines,' says Jim Mendolia. Although he says that 'squid and octopus are actually better frozen because the tissue breaks down.'

'Eventually fresh fish is going to be so hard to get wild because of all the fishery restrictions – there are less boats fishing. It's all going to be farmed or imported frozen,' says Jim. 'And it will be a luxury to eat fresh fish.'

SARDE ALLA BECCAFICO
STUFFED SARDINES

FROM ROSA MITCHELL

16 sardines, scaled
2 cups fresh breadcrumbs
1 cup flat-leaf parsley leaves
½ garlic clove
½ cup freshly grated
    parmesan
1 egg, beaten
salt and pepper
75 g (½ cup) plain flour
olive oil

This is a dish of butterflied sardines sandwiched with a breadcrumb, parsley and parmesan stuffing. The plump stuffed fish with their tails sticking out are said to resemble the *beccafico*, a little bird found in Italy that loves to eat figs (*fico*).

Remove the head and innards of each sardine (you may be able to do this in one action by pulling the head downwards; the innards should come too). Run your thumb from the gut cavity down to the tail to butterfly the sardines (opening them out flat). Pull out the backbones.

Put the breadcrumbs, parsley and garlic in a food processor and process finely. Place in a bowl with the parmesan, egg and salt and pepper and mix well.

Place a sardine in the palm of your hand skin-side down and put a table-spoon of breadcrumb stuffing in the centre. Flatten it out across the sardine without going right to the edges. Place another sardine on top and press it lightly to the stuffing. Repeat with the remaining sardines and stuffing.

Place the flour in a bowl and season with a little salt and pepper. Lightly dust the stuffed sardines in flour. Heat some oil in a frying pan and fry the sardines for about 3 minutes on each side, until golden.

Serves 4

'*Bisogna navigare secondo il vento.* (When the wind blows, you must set your sail.)'

CITRUS-CURED KINGFISH

FROM STEFANO DE PIERI

1 side of kingfish
¼ cup salt
3 blood oranges, zested
    and juiced
1 teaspoon fennel seeds,
    ground
1 star anise, ground
sprigs of thyme
extra-virgin olive oil

This is the freshest-tasting antipasto or entree you'll find, and incredibly healthy and low-fat too (two words you don't often hear in the Italian heartland!). Stefano is surrounded by citrus groves in his inland city of Mildura. Any orange can be used, but his choice is the beautiful blood orange of winter. You may like to serve these delicate slices of fish with a fennel and orange salad (page xxx), and with crusty bread.

Clean the blood line from the fish and remove the pin bones with tweezers. Place the fish in a large dish skin-side down and sprinkle with half the salt, followed by the orange zest, fennel, star anise and thyme. Pour on the orange juice and scatter with the remaining salt. Cover with plastic wrap and refrigerate for 24 hours.

Scrape the flavourings from the fish and slice finely. Drizzle with extra-virgin olive oil.

Serves 8

'Never start fishing, use a net or start a new venture on a Friday.'
Claude Basile

LEATHERJACKET WITH TOMATO, CAPERS, OLIVES AND BREADCRUMBS

FROM ARMANDO PERCUOCO

4 large leatherjackets, heads removed and skinned
100 ml olive oil
3 onions, sliced
3 garlic cloves, peeled
30 black olives, stoned and halved
3 tablespoons salted baby capers, soaked in water for 1 hour and drained
12 ripe roma tomatoes, chopped
salt and pepper
⅓ cup pine nuts, toasted (optional)
1 cup fresh breadcrumbs
handful of flat-leaf parsley, chopped

What a joy to find a recipe for one of the most delicious and consistently cheapest fish in the market. The filleted leatherjackets are baked in the oven with a tomato, olive, caper and pine nut sauce, which is beautifully sweet from lots of caramelised onion.

Fillet the leatherjackets and remove any bones with tweezers.

Heat 2 tablespoons of the oil in a frying pan and fry the onion and garlic cloves until golden and caramelised. Add the olives and capers and fry for 1 minute. Add the tomato and cook for 7 minutes on low heat. Taste for seasoning and add salt or pepper if required. Stir in the pine nuts if using.

Add 125 ml of warm water, increase the heat and cook for 2 minutes. Remove and discard the garlic.

Preheat the oven to 180°C. Pour the remaining oil onto a tray. Set the tray over low heat on the stovetop to heat the oil. Place the leatherjacket fillets on the tray and fry for 30 seconds on each side. Spoon over the tomato mixture and sprinkle with the breadcrumbs, then bake in the oven for approximately 8 minutes, until the breadcrumbs are lightly brown. Scatter with the parsley and serve.

Serves 4

'Chi dorme non piglia pesce.
(He who sleeps catches no fish.)'

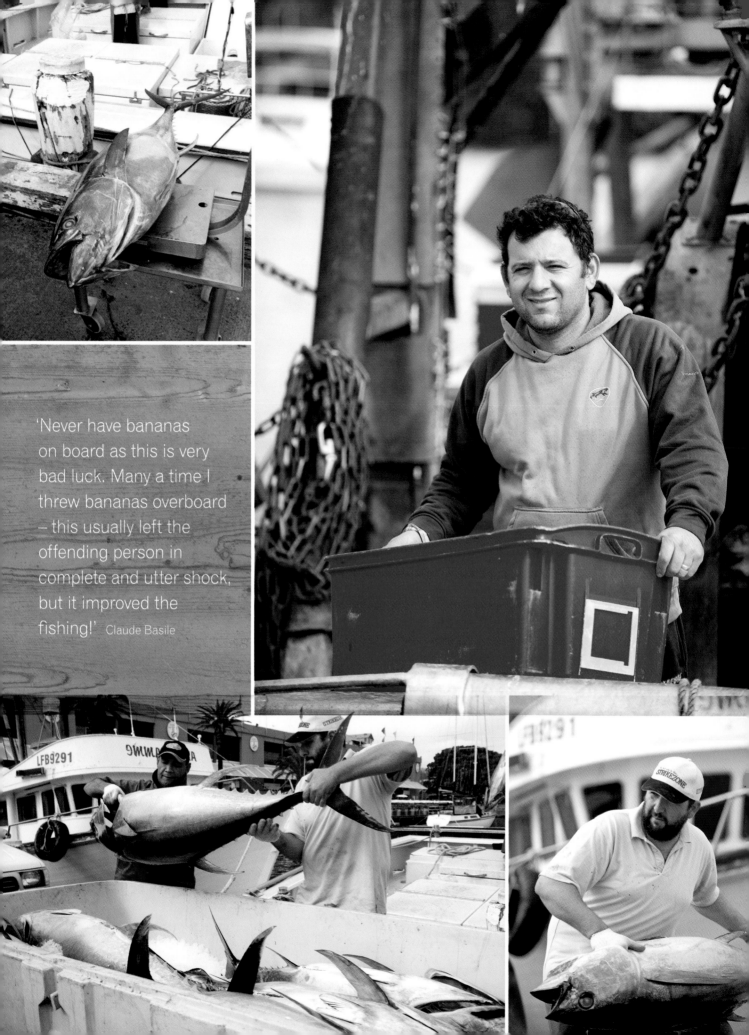

'Never have bananas on board as this is very bad luck. Many a time I threw bananas overboard – this usually left the offending person in complete and utter shock, but it improved the fishing!' Claude Basile

BAKED SNAPPER WITH PARSLEY, CHILLI AND OREGANO

FROM ROBERT CASTELLANI

2 kg snapper, cleaned
   and scaled
salt and pepper
100 ml olive oil
pinch of dried chilli flakes
pinch of dried oregano
1 tablespoon finely chopped
   flat-leaf parsley

This delicious snapper is propped up on its belly on the tray and brushed with a mixture of oil and herbs. A coin is traditionally popped into the mouth of the fish to thank God.

Preheat the oven to 180°C. Score the skin of the snapper in a crisscross pattern and season well with salt and pepper, rubbing into the skin and cavity.

Scrunch up some baking paper and insert it into the cavity. This should allow you to stand the snapper on its belly on a tray. Mix the oil with the chilli and herbs and brush the snapper with three-quarters of this mixture. Bake the snapper for 30–40 minutes, then remove from the oven and brush with the remaining oil before serving.

Serves 4–6

'When I built my boat it was not allowed to leave the builder's shed until the crucifix or a holy picture was placed on board.' Claude Basile

VONGOLE CON CIME DI RAPA IN PADELLA

BABY CLAMS WITH PAN-FRIED BROCCOLI RABE

FROM STEFANO MANFREDI

500 g vongole (baby clams)
3 slices of stale country bread,
 cut into 2 cm cubes
100 ml extra-virgin olive oil
100 ml dry white wine
2 long red chillies, finely sliced
2 large garlic cloves, crushed
3 shallots, finely sliced
1 small leek, finely sliced
200 g broccoli rabe, roughly
 chopped
salt and pepper

Soak the vongole in cold water for 12 hours to purge them of any sand or grit, and wash them under running water.

Put the bread on a tray and toss with 2 tablespoons of the oil. Bake in a 150°C oven for 8–10 minutes, until toasted.

Put the vongole in a saucepan and pour in the wine. Put a lid on the pan, set it over high heat and bring to the boil. Cook, shaking the pan every now and then, until the vongole open (around 2–3 minutes).

Meanwhile, heat the remaining oil in a frying pan and gently fry the chilli, garlic, shallots and leek for a few minutes until tender. Turn up the heat and add the broccoli rabe, stirring well. Season with salt and pepper and cook until the broccoli rabe is tender (about 4–5 minutes). Spoon onto a serving plate, top with the warm vongole (still in their shells) and scatter with the toasted bread.

Serves 4–6

'*Meno pregiato è il pesce, meglio il brodo riesce.* (The less expensive the fish the better the soup.)'

GNOCCHI CON ASTICE
GNOCCHI WITH CRAYFISH

FROM MAURICE ESPOSITO

GNOCCHI
500 g desiree potatoes,
    peeled and cut in half
1 egg
1 teaspoon salt
120 g plain flour

CRAYFISH AND STOCK
1 live crayfish weighing
    approximately 600 g
olive oil
1 carrot, diced
1 celery stalk, diced
1 onion, diced
1 fennel bulb, sliced
1 leek, sliced
2 garlic cloves, finely chopped
2 thyme sprigs
1 bay leaf
500 ml dry white wine
250 ml fish stock

TO FINISH
olive oil
1 garlic clove, finely chopped
pinch of saffron threads
3 ripe roma tomatoes, peeled
    and chopped to a pulp
salmon roe
chervil leaves

To make the gnocchi, boil the potatoes until soft. Drain them and pass through a potato ricer or food mill, and then through a very fine sieve. (If you don't have both pieces of equipment, you can make do with just one or the other, but the lightest gnocchi results from using both.) Leave to cool to room temperature.

Mound the potato on a work surface and add the egg and salt. Add a little flour at a time and lightly mix it in with your hands to form a soft, smooth dough that isn't too sticky. Roll the dough into thin logs (you might need to lightly dust the dough with flour) and cut into 2 cm pieces. To create the classic gnocchi shape, roll the pieces over a ridged butter paddle.

To cook the gnocchi, bring a large saucepan of salted water to the boil, and have a bowl of iced water ready. Carefully add the gnocchi to the boiling water and cook until they rise to the top. Scoop out with a slotted spoon and immerse in cold water. Set aside.

Bring another large saucepan of water to the boil, with another bowl of iced water ready. Put the crayfish in the boiling water for 10 seconds, then lift it out and immediately immerse in the iced water. This blanching helps to separate the meat from the shell.

Once the crayfish has cooled down completely, split it in half lengthwise and remove the flesh. Cut the flesh into 2 cm pieces (the same size as the gnocchi) and set aside.

Heat some olive oil in a saucepan and sauté the carrot, celery, onion, fennel, leek, garlic and herbs until beginning to soften and colour. Add the head and shells of the crayfish and sauté for a further 2 minutes. Add the wine and boil until reduced by half, then pour in the fish stock and simmer for 15 minutes. Strain the stock into a clean saucepan and set it over low heat to keep the stock hot.

To serve, heat some olive oil in a frying pan and lightly sauté the garlic and saffron. Add the crayfish and sauté until lightly coloured (about 2 minutes), then add about ⅓ cup of the stock and the chopped tomato. Stir briefly. Drain the gnocchi and gently fold into the sauce to warm through. Spoon onto plates and garnish with salmon roe and torn chervil leaves.

Serves 4

SCAMPI CON FREGOLA

SCAMPI WITH FREGOLA

FROM SALVATORE PEPE

100 g dried cannellini beans

400 g vongole (baby clams)

2 garlic cloves, 1 peeled and
left whole, 1 finely chopped

300 g fregola

extra-virgin olive oil

400 g scampi

1 small red chilli, finely
chopped

100 g ripe roma tomatoes or
cherry tomatoes, chopped

2 large handfuls rocket

salt

This is not a traditional dish, but one Salvatore loves to cook. It combines luxurious scampi and vongole with two peasant foods – cannellini beans and fregola, a small, round pasta with a nutty flavour from being lightly roasted. As Salvatore says, the flavours really work together and this is a dish fit for any special occasion.

Soak the beans overnight. Soak the vongole in cold water for 12 hours to purge them of any sand or grit, and wash them under running water.

Drain and rinse the beans, then put into a saucepan with the whole garlic clove and cover with fresh water. Simmer until soft, then leave to cool in the cooking water (to stop the skins splitting).

Cook the fregola in a pot of salted boiling water until al dente. Drain and toss with a little oil to stop it sticking together.

Cut the scampi in half lengthways using a sharp knife or kitchen scissors. Rinse under running water and drain on paper towel.

Heat a splash of oil in a large saucepan and fry the chopped garlic and chilli until golden. Add the tomato, cover with a lid and cook until soft. Add the scampi, vongole and rocket and cook, shaking the pan from time to time, until the vongole shells open (this should only take a few minutes). Add the drained beans and fregola and stir through. Season with salt to taste. Serve drizzled with extra-virgin olive oil.

Serves 4

CALAMARI RIPIENE
STUFFED CALAMARI

FROM GUY GROSSI

CALAMARI
500 g picked, cooked
    mud-crab meat
1 teaspoon finely chopped
    coriander
1 teaspoon finely chopped
    flat-leaf parsley
¼ teaspoon smoked paprika
grated zest of 1 lemon
¼ long red chilli, finely
    chopped
splash of olive oil
sea salt
freshly ground black pepper
12 cleaned baby calamari
    tubes

TO SERVE
2 tablespoons basil seeds
sea salt
1 small cucumber, peeled
    and finely diced
1 teaspoon smoked paprika
extra-virgin olive oil
baccala mantecato from
    page 24 (optional)
black-olive tapenade
    (optional)
baby herbs (optional)
oven-dried roma tomatoes
    (optional)

This is an elegant way of serving calamari, stuffed with mud-crab meat, herbs, lemon and spices.

Combine the crab meat, herbs, paprika, lemon zest, chilli and oil in a bowl and season with salt and pepper.

Stuff the mixture into the calamari tubes until three-quarters full. Firmly wrap each tube in plastic wrap, twisting the ends shut.

To prepare the garnishes, mix some basil seeds with a pinch of salt and a little water and set aside to soften for a few minutes, then drain. Combine the cucumber, paprika and a drizzle of oil in a separate bowl.

Steam the stuffed calamari for 3–4 minutes.

Place a spoonful of cucumber salad and baccala mantecato (if using) on each plate. Drizzle with tapenade (if using) and scatter with basil seeds. Remove the warm calamari from the plastic and place on top. If you wish, finish by scattering with baby herbs and adding a few pieces of oven-dried tomato.

Serves 4

'If you have something to say, head for the kitchen, because that is where everything happens.'

PASTA MAKING

The Italians have fabulous descriptions to describe their cooking processes. When it comes to pasta, there are sayings like '*la condiche la pasta*', meaning 'dress it but don't have it swimming'. Or the now-famous term 'al dente' translating as 'to the tooth', meaning the pasta still has a bit of bite to it. To judge al dente by eye, a strand of spaghetti should still have a little white centre.

Cooking the pasta to the desired stage is a question that engages whole families, and can be the spark that ignites wars! Some families have a democratic system, like Nino Zoccali's family. 'In our family it usually took about three people to determine whether the pasta was cooked to the proper level of "doneness" or not … Quite a ritual, really, reflecting on it, though we didn't give it a second thought at the time; it was just what we did.'

Others know exactly how they like their pasta cooked and demand it every time. Danny Russo says his mother won't let him cook dried pasta. 'She tells me that I just wave the pasta over the boiling water and into the plate – she doesn't like it so al dente!'

For restaurateur Lucio Galetto, it's the opposite: he loves it 'in piedi' – standing up – even more al dente! And Daniel Airo-Farulla says his family's pasta was also cooked very al dente – just the way his father liked it. 'If it wasn't like this, he wasn't happy for the rest of the night!'

Timing is all important in serving dinner too, so when the pasta is being dropped into the boiling water, households ring with the phrase shouted from the kitchen, 'Butta la pasta', meaning 'I'm putting on the pasta so you better finish what you're doing and get to the table otherwise you'll miss out!' A forceful Italian mamma and a hungry family is an incredibly motivating force.

Some tips from Italians on cooking pasta can come in handy. 'Always taste your pasta water once you've salted it so you are sure it has the right level of salt,' says Eugenio Maiale. And Guy Grossi says: 'The water must be boiling vigorously, and there should be plenty of it. Never put too much pasta into a small pot.'

There's something about making pasta from scratch that is so levelling and such a good tonic. Flour, salt, eggs. Mixed gradually by hand and kneaded into a dough. Rested. Fed into a pasta machine and rolled to work the glutens in the flour and

make the dough elastic. Turning the settings down to produce a thinner and thinner sheet. And then, the joy of cutting the shapes you need – silky ribbons of pappardelle or fettucine, or long sheets dotted with fillings to be cut into ravioli.

Homemade pasta is Graziella Alessi's favourite recipe learnt from her mother. 'Her *pasta al forno* [baked pasta] was made with fresh pasta and I'd love walking into the kitchen, seeing pasta laid out over the kitchen table, ready to be dropped into the pot. Mum would always make extra and have it hanging over wooden rods, drying out. It was like a forest of pasta! My mother would use eggs from our own chickens to make the pasta, and naturally the *sugo*, or sauce, would come from tomatoes grown in our backyard.'

The right flour is crucial to making great pasta says Guy Grossi. 'You need flour that is fresh and of very high quality, and well milled. Flour varies a lot from different millers and freshness is very important because the flavour that we taste in the pasta is actually the flour. The key, after that, is high-quality, fresh eggs.'

Guy's rule: Never use ordinary cake flour for pasta, because you need a strong flour. He says to try '00' flour, an Italian strong flour that is great for pizza and bread and fine, too, if you are just making a little bit of pasta to be used immediately at home. However, the top flour for pasta is durum wheat flour, which gives a wonderful textural bite. 'The Italians call that "*la farina duro*", which means golden flour – that's the best.'

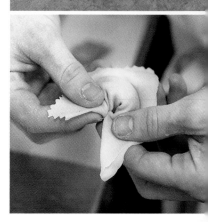

PASTA FRESCA
FRESH PASTA

FROM GUY GROSSI

250 g unbleached plain flour
250 g durum wheat flour
pinch of salt
4 eggs

Sift the flours and salt into a bowl. Add the eggs and use your hands to gradually incorporate them into the flour. Add a little water if required – the dough should be soft but not sticky. (Alternatively, you can mix the dough in a food processor.) Transfer to a work surface and knead for a few minutes, then cover with plastic wrap and leave to rest for 30 minutes.

Divide the dough into 2 or 3 pieces so it is easier to work with. Take the first piece and roll it through a pasta machine on the widest setting. Fold it in half and run it through the machine again. Do this several times – this process is called laminating and should make the dough silky and smooth. Now you can start rolling the pasta out at narrower settings. Keep going until the sheet is 1–2 mm thick.

Lay the sheet on a floured surface while you roll out the other pieces of dough. Cut the sheets into desired shapes and spread on a floured tray until you are ready to cook the pasta (it is best cooked the same day, or it can be frozen).

Makes 600 g fresh pasta

'*Chi impasta senza fretta la farina fa la pasta più gustosa e fina*'. (Those who knead the dough without haste make the pasta tastier and fine.)

LASAGNE

FROM GUY GROSSI

SUGO BOLOGNESE
2½ tablespoons olive oil
1 large onion, finely chopped
2 garlic cloves, finely chopped
1 small red chilli, finely chopped
4 cloves, ground
a little freshly grated nutmeg
800 g minced beef
100 g minced pork
100 g minced chicken
1 sprig of rosemary, leaves
    picked and chopped
1 tablespoon chopped sage
handful of flat-leaf parsley
    leaves, chopped
2 bay leaves
handful of basil leaves,
    crushed to a paste with a
    little olive oil
200 g tomato paste
200 ml red wine
2 litres chicken or veal stock,
    or water
sea salt
freshly ground black pepper

BESCIAMELLA (BECHAMEL SAUCE)
80 g butter
80 g plain flour
1 litre milk
½ small onion, roughly chopped
1 bay leaf
1 clove
a little freshly grated nutmeg
sea salt
ground white pepper

fresh lasagne sheets for
    6 or more layers (page 125)
olive oil
250 g parmigiano reggiano,
    grated

This is Guy's mother's recipe, which he serves in his restaurant. Diners keep on coming back for it.

To make the *sugo* bolognese, heat the olive oil in a pot over medium heat and sauté the onion, garlic, chilli, ground cloves and nutmeg for 4–5 minutes, until soft and lightly caramelised. Add the meat and continue to cook, stirring, for 5 minutes. Add the herbs, including the basil paste, and continue to stir until the meat is well browned and broken up finely (about another 5 minutes). Add the tomato paste and cook for another 1–2 minutes, stirring constantly to prevent sticking. Pour in the wine and boil to reduce by half. Add the stock or water and season with salt and pepper. Bring to the boil then reduce the heat and simmer gently for 1 hour, stirring occasionally and adding more water if required.

To make the *besciamella*, melt the butter in a heavy-based saucepan over medium heat and add the flour. Stir with a wooden spoon until the mixture forms a smooth paste. Cook, stirring constantly, for 2–4 minutes, taking care not to let the paste colour. Remove from the heat and leave to cool.

Put the milk, onion, bay leaf, clove and nutmeg in another saucepan and heat gently until simmering. Remove from the heat and leave for 15 minutes to allow the flavours to infuse.

Strain the warm milk onto the cooled paste and whisk together. Bring to the boil, whisking vigorously to avoid lumps, then reduce the heat to low and simmer for 10 minutes. Season with salt and white pepper.

Cook the lasagne sheets in salted boiling water until al dente. Drain and put into a bowl of cold water with a few drops of olive oil to prevent the sheets from sticking together.

Preheat the oven to 180°C. Ladle a small amount of *sugo* into a large baking dish and cover with a layer of lasagne sheets. Ladle more *sugo* over the sheets and drizzle over some *besciamella*, then sprinkle with grated parmigiano reggiano. Continue to layer in this way until you reach the top of the dish (aim for at least 6 layers of lasagne). Add the grated cheese every second layer. Finish with a layer of cheese. Bake for 30–40 minutes.

Serve with a little extra *sugo* and more parmigiano reggiano if desired.

Serves 6–8

PECORA IN CAPPOTTO CON FREGOLA
MUTTON STEW WITH FREGOLA

FROM GIOVANNI PILU

1 mutton shoulder on the
  bone, cut into large chunks
  by your butcher
6 roma tomatoes, cut into
  wedges
1 tablespoon salt
3 onions, halved
3 carrots, cut into 5 cm chunks
3 celery stalks, cut into 5 cm
  chunks
4 potatoes, peeled and halved
300 g fregola

'Pecora in cappotto' translates to 'sheep in a jacket' – the 'jacket' being the potatoes and onions that cloak the meat.

Fregola is a small ball-shaped pasta from Sardinia with a nutty flavour from being lightly roasted. It can be found at good Italian delis.

Put the mutton pieces, tomato and salt in a pot and cover with cold water. Bring to the boil and skim the surface. Lower the heat and simmer for 1½–2 hours or until the meat begins to fall from the bone. Add the onion, carrot, celery and potato and cook until the vegetables are soft. Remove the meat and vegetables from the stock and keep warm.

Return the stock to the boil and add the fregola. Cook for approximately 8 minutes, until al dente.

The minestra, or soup, is served as a first course followed by the meat and vegetables.

Serves 6

'Amicizie e pasta, sono meglio caldi.
(Friendship and pasta are best warm.)'

'If I'm drying my pasta, I hang it over a clothes horse or something like that, and then I just leave it in a spot where it's not too draughty but the air is still moving so there's no moisture.' Guy Grossi

SPAGHETTI CON PATATE E CAVOLO NERO

SPAGHETTI WITH POTATO AND CAVOLO NERO

FROM LINA SICILIANO

salt
2 small potatoes, roughly
    chopped
2 bunches cavolo nero,
    roughly chopped
150 g dried medium-thick
    spaghetti (no. 8)
125 ml extra-virgin olive oil,
    plus extra for drizzling
2 garlic cloves, peeled

Bring 3 litres of water to the boil in a pot. Salt the water. Add the potatoes and cook for 15 minutes. After 5 minutes, add the cavolo nero (to cook for 10 minutes). Break the bunch of spaghetti into 3 short lengths and add to the pot to cook according to the time stated on the packet, cooking until al dente.

Meanwhile, heat the oil in a saucepan and sauté the garlic cloves.

Drain the potato, cavolo nero and spaghetti, reserving a cup of cooking water. Add the vegetables and pasta to the oil and garlic and stir. Add some cooking water if the pasta seems dry. Serve immediately, drizzling with more oil, alongside some crusty bread.

Serves 2

'Pasta is always a first course – "*E per il secondo, che c' è*? (And what's for second course?)" My family is never content with just a pasta meal!' Rosa Matto

PAPPARDELLE WITH DUCK RAGU

FROM FRED PIZZINI

DUCK STOCK

1 duck, carcass only (meat
   reserved for the ragu)
1 onion, roughly chopped
1 celery stalk, roughly
   chopped
1 carrot, roughly chopped
2 star anise
sprigs of rosemary, sage,
   tarragon and thyme

RAGU

meat from the duck
1 kg tomatoes, peeled,
   seeded and diced
juice of ½ lemon
1 tablespoon sugar
3 tablespoons olive oil
3 tablespoons butter
1 onion, diced
4 garlic cloves, chopped
2 bay leaves
handful of basil and
   flat-leaf parsley leaves
a few sprigs of thyme
   and rosemary
salt and pepper

500g pasta dough (page 125)
grated pecorino to serve

It doesn't get better than this – a rich, full-flavoured ragu of duck tossed with ribbons of perfect fresh pasta. The ragu begins by making a quick duck stock to add to the rich tomato sauce as it simmers (leftover stock can be used for soup or risotto). Serve this dish with a simple radicchio salad.

To make the stock, first remove the duck meat from the bones. Pull each leg out from the bird and slice through the skin to expose the flesh. Twist the legs up and out and cut through the joint. Cut the legs into thighs and drumsticks and cut the meat from the bones. To remove each breast, cut alongside the breastbone and slowly work your way down and across to cut off the meat. Trim the excess skin and fat from all of the meat. Cut the meat into small bite-sized pieces and set aside for the ragu.

Place the bones in a large saucepan with just enough water to cover. Add the remaining ingredients and simmer for 1 hour, skimming off the fat occasionally.

To make the ragu, put the diced tomato in a colander set over a bowl. Pour over the lemon juice and sprinkle with the sugar, and allow the juices to drain into the bowl for 30 minutes. This will intensify the flavour of the tomatoes.

Heat half the oil and butter in a large saucepan and fry the onion and garlic until beginning to caramelise. Add the drained tomatoes and herbs. Season with salt and pepper and simmer for 1½ hours, adding a little duck stock and drained tomato juice occasionally to keep the sauce runny.

Gently heat the remaining oil and butter in a frying pan and brown the chopped duck. Add to the tomato sauce and simmer for a further 30 minutes, adding more stock and tomato juice as needed. The sauce should be rich and moist.

Meanwhile, finish the pasta. Divide the dough into a few pieces so it is easier to work with. Roll the first piece through a pasta machine on the widest setting. Fold it in half and run it through the machine again. Do this several times until smooth, then start rolling it out at narrower settings until it is around 2 mm thick. Lay the sheet on a floured surface while you roll out the other pieces of dough.

Fold the sheets up a few times (this makes them easier to cut straight) and cut into strips roughly 2 cm wide. Unravel the ribbons of pasta and cut into shorter lengths if needed. Boil in a pot of salted water until al dente, then drain, return to the pot and toss the ragu through the pasta. Serve with grated pecorino.

Serves 6

PASTA E FAGIOLI
PASTA AND BEANS

FROM ARMANDO PERCUOCO

100 g dried cannellini beans
80 ml extra-virgin olive oil,
    plus extra for drizzling
2 garlic cloves, peeled
1 celery stalk, chopped
a few pieces of prosciutto
    rind
1 tomato, chopped
salt and pepper
200 g dried tubetti pasta
45 g parmesan, grated
1 tablespoon finely chopped
    flat-leaf parsley

This is one of the classic dishes from the realm of *cucina povera*, the food of the poor. But it is comfort food that touches your soul no matter who you are – a thick soup of pasta and cannellini beans with lovely hints of prosciutto.

Soak the beans for about 6 hours in a saucepan of water. Drain and replace the water, bring the beans to the boil and simmer until they are soft (about 45 minutes). Drain the beans, keeping the cooking water.

Heat half the oil in a large saucepan and sauté the garlic cloves, celery and prosciutto rind for about 5 minutes. Add the tomato, beans and 250 ml of the bean cooking water. Bring to the boil, then remove from the heat and pick out the garlic cloves and prosciutto rind. Season to taste.

Cook the tubetti in salted boiling water until a little under al dente. Drain and add to the soup. Return the soup to a simmer, add the remaining oil and cook for another 3 minutes. If the soup seems too thick, add more bean water.

Serve sprinkled with parmesan and parsley and drizzled with more oil.

Serves 4 as an entree

'I fagioli sono la carne dei poveri.
(Beans are the meat of the poor.)'

SPAGHETTI ALLE VONGOLE
SPAGHETTI WITH BABY CLAMS

FROM EUGENIO MAIALE

1.4 kg vongole (baby clams)
450 g dried spaghetti
220 ml extra-virgin olive oil
1 heaped tablespoon
    chopped garlic
½ teaspoon chopped red
    chilli
salt
100 ml dry white wine such
    as pinot grigio
½ cup chopped flat-leaf
    parsley

Eugenio grew up on the coast and spent time on the sand raking for the sweet little shells that make this simple dish so marvellous. The secret is in the timing – starting to cook the vongole just after the water for the pasta comes to the boil.

Soak the vongole in cold water for 12 hours to purge them of any sand or grit. Wash them under running water (Eugenio washes them 3 times).

Bring a pot of salted water to the boil and add the spaghetti, cooking until al dente.

Just after adding the pasta, heat 120 ml of the olive oil in a large heavy-based frying pan over medium–high heat. When hot, add the vongole, garlic and chilli and turn the heat to high. Stir once or twice as the vongole begin to cook. When around half of the vongole have opened, season with salt to taste and add the wine. Simmer briefly. Add the remaining oil and parsley.

Drain the spaghetti and toss through the vongole. Serve immediately.

Serves 4

'Health flows from the happiness
of the heart.'

SPAGHETTI AGLIO E OLIO
SPAGHETTI WITH GARLIC AND OLIVE OIL

FROM GUY GROSSI

500 g dried spaghetti
100 ml extra-virgin olive oil
2 garlic cloves, finely chopped
pinch of chopped red chilli
1 teaspoon capers
4 anchovy fillets, torn
(optional)
sea salt and freshly ground
black pepper
½ cup chopped flat-leaf
parsley

This is the simplest of pasta dishes; besides garlic and oil Guy adds a touch of chilli, capers and anchovies. It's Italian fast food, so you can get home after a long day or a late night and it's ready in a moment.

Cook the spaghetti in a large pot of well-salted boiling water until al dente. Meanwhile, heat the olive oil in a large frying pan over medium heat and add the garlic, chilli, capers and anchovies (if using). Season to taste with salt and pepper. Cook over medium heat for a few minutes without letting the garlic colour too much. Drain the pasta and add it to the frying pan. Add the parsley and toss well. Serve immediately.

Serves 4

'*Chi adopera l'aglio non fa mai sbaglio.* (Those who use garlic never make a mistake.)'

CHEESE

Cheese is an essential part of Italian cuisine, adding luscious texture and flavour to salads and antipasto; finishing touches to main courses; fillings for *cannoli* and cakes; and enjoyed with fruit to finish a meal.

'There's never a part of the day when we don't eat cheese,' says Giorgio Linguanti, a specialist cheese-maker or '*casaro*' – a keeper of secrets, traditions and knowledge. He says everyone in southern Italy starts their day with cheese: 'In Sicily, where I come from, you can start early in the morning with a soft *cannoli* filled with sweet ricotta accompanying your coffee, or have a nice *panino* for breakfast with tomato, prosciutto and mozzarella. This is really pretty standard,' he says with pride.

'Then Italian lunches – they are very generous and in the more simple dishes like pasta we never miss a nice handful of grated cheese (caciocavallo, pecorino, or even *ricotta salata*), and so it goes on.' Giorgio jokes that his mother would put cheese in everything the family ate. 'My mum, she was putting cheese in meatballs, stuffed calamari, schnitzel, arancini, pizza, pasta and nearly even in my socks!'

Ricotta is important in many Italian households, says specialist cheese providore or 'formaggiaio' John Buonavoglia. 'On Sunday mornings, Italian people come with their containers from home to pick up warm ricotta from our factory – just as it's made,' he says. 'But it's important for them that we include the whey. Apparently it is loved for "keeping you regular" and it's eaten with ricotta in the same way people eat porridge – eaten warm for breakfast with honey.'

The art of making the soft white cheeses – bocconcini and mozzarella, caciotta, burrata and ricotta – has been handed down through families and small businesses, with great milk being the key to exquisite flavour.

Giorgio Linguanti says he looks forward to work every morning. 'The magic for me is the moment when the milk starts to coagulate, starting the cheese-making process,' he says. 'It's my favourite moment because you touch the milk, you feel, you smell – a moment full of sensation – and also because most of the time it's only myself early in the morning.'

While the French pride themselves on exceptional cheeses across their many regions, Italy has its own very distinguished regional cheeses, including those using the high-protein buffalo milk. Buffalo mozzarella has a richness, silkiness and pure-white colour that sets it apart. Buffalo milk is also used to make hard cheese with great depth of flavour.

Amongst the aged hard cheeses, the 'king' is parmigiano reggiano. Grana padano follows closely behind, being the parmesan many people choose to have on pasta.

As John Buonavoglia says, parmigiano reggiano – with its salty little crystals or diamonds of flavour – should be savoured and eaten as is. In Italy you'd be 'locked up' for grating it on your pasta!

'*La boca le mia strnca se la sa mia de aca.* (In dialect: The mouth is not tired if it does not taste like cow, meaning you must have cheese to finish every meal!)'

CAPRESE SALAD

FROM GUY GROSSI

vine-ripened tomatoes,
   finely sliced
buffalo mozzarella,
   finely sliced
basil leaves
red onion, finely diced
good-quality white-wine
   vinegar
extra-virgin olive oil
sea salt
freshly ground black pepper
baby capers
dried oregano

This is a simple summer salad, and with the addition of crusty bread, it can be a meal on its own.

To assemble the salad, lay slices of tomato on a flat serving dish. Top each slice with a slice of mozzarella and then a basil leaf. Each ingredient should be visible, creating layers of red, white and green. Scatter with some onion and dress with vinegar and olive oil. Sprinkle with salt, pepper, capers and oregano.

'My mum always blesses the milk when making ricotta cheese, but then crosses her fingers so that if God doesn't help then luck might!'

SPINACH GNOCCHETTI

FROM KATRINA PIZZINI

500 g spinach
3 tablespoons chopped
    flat-leaf parsley
1 tablespoon chopped
    oregano
    (or 1 teaspoon dried)
1 tablespoon chopped thyme
    (or 1 teaspoon dried)
3 eggs plus 2 egg yolks
350 g plain flour
⅓ teaspoon ground nutmeg
¼ teaspoon ground white
    pepper
1 teaspoon salt
150 ml cream
100 g parmesan, shaved
    or grated
100 g sharp blue-vein cheese,
    roughly chopped

Katrina's baby spinach gnocchi are a beautiful shade of green, flavoured with herbs and nutmeg, then layered in a dish with the delicious additions of cream, parmesan and blue cheese.

Katrina learnt to make pasta from her husband's family, who come from northern Italy not far from Austria as the crow flies. She uses a spatzle maker for the *gnocchetti*, as Austrian and German cooks do. A spatzle maker looks like a grater with a sliding square cup attached to the top. The dough goes into the cup, which is slid back and forth to push the dough through the holes of the grater into a pot of boiling water. You can also use a potato ricer (for smaller *gnocchetti*) or even a piping bag with a small nozzle, and swirl the bag over the water. Serve this with a radicchio salad and some crusty bread.

Bring a saucepan of water to the boil and cook the spinach for 3 minutes. Drain and leave to cool, then squeeze out the excess moisture (you should be left with approximately 400 g of spinach).

Put the spinach in a food processor and process until mushy. Add the herbs and process for another 30 seconds, then add the eggs and egg yolks and process briefly.

Transfer to a bowl and stir in the flour, nutmeg, pepper and salt to make a dough with a gooey consistency. Cover and refrigerate for 30 minutes.

Bring a pot of water to the boil. Rub half the spinach dough through a spatzle maker into the pot. Simmer the *gnocchetti* for 5 minutes, then scoop out with a slotted spoon into a colander. Leave to drain for a minute before transferring to a serving dish. Pour over half the cream and scatter with half of the cheeses. Repeat with the remaining dough, topping with the remaining cream and cheeses.

Lightly mix with a spoon and serve immediately.

Serves 4

'Great milk makes
great cheese.'
John Buonavoglia

RAVIOLI DI PATATE E RICOTTA CON SPECK E CAVOLO NERO

RAVIOLI OF POTATO AND RICOTTA WITH SPECK AND CAVOLO NERO

FROM ANDREW CIBEJ

PASTA
375 g plain flour
100 g strong flour
1 teaspoon salt
200 g eggs (approximately 4 eggs)
50 g egg yolks (approximately 2 egg yolks)
semolina for dusting
beaten egg whites for brushing

FILLING
3 medium potatoes
salt
½ garlic clove, crushed
150 g fresh ricotta
2 tablespoons freshly grated montasio or parmesan
grated zest of ½ lemon
small handful of flat-leaf parsley, finely chopped
pepper

SAUCE
olive oil
2 shallots, finely chopped
100 g speck or pancetta, finely sliced
2 handfuls cavolo nero, roughly chopped
2½ tablespoons white wine
250 ml chicken stock
knob of unsalted butter
50 g freshly grated montasio or parmesan

freshly grated montasio or parmesan to serve

This dish is worth all the work you put in – a magnificent combination of silky pasta with a potato and ricotta filling, tossed with a sauce of speck and cavolo nero.

To make the pasta, put the flours and salt in a bowl. Add the eggs and egg yolks and use your hands to gradually incorporate into the flour and form a dough. (Alternatively, you can mix the dough in a food processor.) Transfer to a work surface and knead for a few minutes, then cover with plastic wrap and leave to rest for at least 30 minutes.

To make the filling, cook the potatoes in salted boiling water. While hot, pass them through a potato ricer, food mill or fine sieve into a bowl. Stir in the remaining ingredients and season to taste.

Divide the pasta dough into a few pieces so it is easier to work with. Take the first piece and roll it through a pasta machine on the widest setting. Fold it in half and run it through the machine again. Do this several times until smooth, then start rolling the pasta out at narrower settings until you reach the second last setting. Lay the sheet on a surface dusted with semolina while you roll out the other pieces of dough.

Place heaped teaspoons of filling at 5 cm intervals along one side of each pasta sheet. Brush egg white around the fillings. Fold over the other sides of the pasta sheets to cover the fillings. Press out any trapped air and cut between each filling to separate into ravioli. Press the edges of each ravioli to seal them shut. Dust with semolina to prevent them sticking to each other.

Bring a large pot of salted water to the boil for the ravioli. Meanwhile, pre-pare the sauce. Heat a little oil in a saucepan over medium heat and sauté the shallots. Add the speck or pancetta and toss briefly, then add the cavolo nero followed by the wine. Allow the wine to reduce completely, then add the stock and simmer for a few minutes. Add the butter and cheese. The consistency of the sauce should be slightly viscous. Taste for seasoning.

Boil the ravioli until they float (about 1 minute). Drain, then toss them through the sauce. Spoon onto plates and scatter with grated montasio or parmesan.

Serves 6–8

TRENETTE WITH PESTO, POTATO AND GREEN BEANS

FROM LUCIO GALETTO

PESTO
1 garlic clove
pinch of sea salt
40 small–medium basil leaves, washed and patted dry
1 tablespoon pine nuts
2 tablespoons freshly grated parmesan
1 tablespoon freshly grated mild pecorino
approximately 120 ml extra-virgin olive oil

1 large waxy potato such as desiree, peeled and diced
300 g green beans, sliced
400 g dried trenette (or linguine)
knob of butter
freshly grated parmesan

Simplicity and freshness – Lucio shows us how to make a proper Ligurian pesto, which is said to be the best, creamiest pesto in Italy. This combination of pesto, potato and green beans with trenette (a long pasta similar to linguine) is a classic dish from the region.

To make proper Ligurian pesto, you have to use a mortar and pestle. Place the garlic, salt (which helps to keep the basil green) and basil in the mortar and start crushing. You shouldn't pound the basil, but rather press the pestle around the sides of the mortar in a circular motion so that the ingredients meld smoothly together. Add the pine nuts (raw, not toasted) and the cheeses and keep pressing until the ingredients are blended to a paste. Transfer to a bowl and add the oil – as much as the pesto will absorb – mixing with a wooden spoon.

Alternatively, you can make the pesto in a blender. Place the ingredients in the blender and process on the lowest speed, and pulse every now and then, until the sauce is creamy.

If you are not using the pesto immediately, pour a layer of oil over the surface to prevent discolouration.

Bring 3 litres of salted water to boil in a pot. Add the potato first and cook for 12 minutes. Add the beans 5 minutes after the potato, to cook for 7 minutes. Add the pasta to cook according to the time stated on the packet, cooking until al dente. Drain, reserving 2 tablespoons of cooking water.

Put half the pesto in a large bowl. Add the cooking water, potatoes, beans and pasta, and the butter, and toss well. Spoon the rest of the pesto on top, sprinkle with parmesan and serve immediately.

Serves 4

COOKING AT HOME

Italian food is basically home food. You may get fancier looking dishes in restaurants, but their soul comes from recipes passed down through the generations. 'We don't have haute cuisine in Italy – it's all from the family,' explains Stefano Manfredi. 'Once dishes go into the kitchens of restaurants, things change subtly in terms of presentation, but they're essentially the same thing.' And the keepers of those traditional dishes are the mothers and grandmothers: 'They're who we've learnt everything from.'

Some lessons only sink in later in life. Graziella Alessi says she 'got it' years later. 'When I think about my childhood, looking over my mother's shoulder as she cooked, the question I always found myself asking her was, "How much of that do you put in?" And the answer always seemed frustratingly vague!

'It wasn't until I got my hands in there and started cooking myself that I actually began to understand what my mother was talking about. Cooking's not just about following a written recipe; it's about feeling what's going on with your food.'

Simplicity is the key, and keeping it simple can grow out of necessity – of having no choice but to use what is available and to make it special. 'My nonna grew up during the wars. There was a lot of poverty so they had to survive on very little,'says Susie (aka Assunta) di Censo. 'Nonna can make a wonderful meal with whatever she has in the fridge, even if it's only three ingredients. People call it "cucina povera [the food of the poor]", which came from the way our grandparents and parents grew up. It's very "in" in restaurants now, which is something that my parents and grandparents are unable to fathom!'

Vince Garreffa remembers coming to Australia with very little and his parents doing without to keep the family going. 'My mother obviously understood how precious food was and how hard she worked to prepare it, and her kids had to eat it all and not be spoilt!'

'In our younger years when we were very poor we – the kids – would be eating pasta and meat on the side, while Mum and Dad ate pasta with only butter and cheap grated cheese. As a little boy I thought they were nuts to eat that instead of the pasta with meat. Later it would dawn on me that money was so short they preferred to give the protein to their kids while they made do with the plain pasta.'

Nino Zoccali learnt that he had to be 'at the dinner table on time, and everybody eats everything, no questions asked,' he says. 'It felt a bit harsh at the time but gave us a good appreciation of a range of foods from a very early age. I have done the same with my nine-year-old son, Luca, and people are amazed at the things he loves to eat!'

'What's for dinner?' In Calabrian dialect: *'Aqua cadda cu brocia*! (Hot water with a fork!)'

'Mamma's golden rule at the kitchen table was, "*Mangiatela tutta o t'ammazzo*! (Eat it all or I'll kill you!)"' Vince Garreffa

One tradition that is strong in Italian Australian families is the two-kitchen concept. One is a perfect 'show' kitchen that is never used except to make coffee, and is filled with all the mod cons. 'We are very proud of our show kitchens,' says Rosa Matto. 'We Italians don't like smells in the house and the show kitchen is always clean no matter what!'

The second kitchen is used for everything, and for many families it is found in their garage. 'Dad thought he'd have somewhere to park his car when they moved into their new house as newlyweds, but it was commandeered for a kitchen,' laughs Rosa.

The kitchen is the centre of the universe. 'It was the hub of the household and whenever you needed anything, that's where you went,' remembers Guy Grossi. 'If you had something to say you would go to the kitchen, because that was the room where everything unfolded. And you could smell the cooking from outside on the street – it was always beautiful.'

The care that goes into preparing a meal is never allowed to go unnoticed. Cattle-farmer Daniela Mollica remembers her father teaching his children not to rush their meals. 'Even if it was just an orange and *finocchio* [fennel] salad, he would present it with care so that there was an appreciation of what we were about to eat,' she says. 'He had a phrase "Eat first with your eyes". My father grew up on the islands just north of Sicily (Lipari), which post World War II was terribly poor. I think they yearned to be able eat more than just the bread – which they cooked themselves – and the ricotta – which they were lucky enough to make as they had a goat – so this saying is about gratitude.'

BRODO

1 chicken, cut into 8 pieces
1 celery stalk including leaves,
    roughly chopped
1 medium carrot,
    roughly chopped
1 medium onion,
    roughly chopped
6 flat-leaf parsley sprigs
1 bay leaf
1 tablespoon salt,
    or more to taste
freshly ground black pepper

It's all about the *brodo* (broth). Broth is the base to every good cuisine and every good kitchen. The key to making a beautifully rich *brodo* is to let it cook very slowly and gently.

Put the ingredients other than the salt and pepper in a pot and cover with cold water. Bring to a rolling boil, then skim off any foam and fat that rises to the surface. Lower the heat, add the salt and pepper and simmer for 2½ hours, skimming occasionally. Taste and adjust the salt if necessary. Strain (reserve the chicken for another use, such as pasta or sandwiches) and leave the broth to cool to room temperature, then cover and refrigerate overnight. The next day, skim off any fat that has solidified on the surface.

Makes about 2 litres

'Tutto fa brodo. (Every little bit counts.)'

MINESTRA DI FARRO CON FAGIOLI

FARRO SOUP WITH BEANS

FROM GUY GROSSI

400 g dried borlotti beans,
    soaked overnight
sea salt
125 ml olive oil
1 small onion, finely chopped
2 garlic cloves, lightly bruised
1 carrot, finely sliced
1 celery stalk, finely chopped
200 g pancetta, chopped
3 roma tomatoes, chopped
2 small potatoes, peeled and
    chopped
1 tablespoon chopped sage
freshly ground black pepper
½ cup chopped flat-leaf
    parsley
100 g farro
extra-virgin olive oil for
    drizzling
freshly grated parmigiano
    reggiano or pecorino

This heart-warming Tuscan soup is rich in flavour and texture. Borlotti beans are cooked until soft, then some are pureed and some left whole. Farro, an ancient relative of wheat, is added to the soup like pasta.

Drain and rinse the beans. Put into a large saucepan and add a little salt and enough water to cover the beans. Bring to the boil, then reduce the heat and simmer uncovered for 20 minutes, or until just tender. Drain the beans, reserving the cooking water. Puree half the beans in a blender with some of the cooking water. Set aside the pureed beans, whole beans and remaining cooking water.

Heat the oil in a saucepan over medium heat and add the onion, garlic, carrot, celery and pancetta. Sauté for 3 minutes, then add the tomato, potato and sage and cook for 2 minutes. Season with salt and pepper.

Add the pureed beans and parsley, then stir in the remaining cooking water from the beans and simmer for 20 minutes. Add the whole beans and farro and cook for a further 20 minutes, adding more water if necessary. Serve drizzled with extra-virgin olive oil and offer parmigiano reggiano or pecorino at the table.

Serves 4

'My mother and her mother would never cook pulses in an aluminium pot because it hardened them – always use a wooden spoon and enamel or stainless steel pots.' Rosa Mitchell

STRACCIATELLA ALLA ROMANA

EGG SOUP

FROM GUY GROSSI

1 litre chicken stock
3 eggs
100 g parmigiano reggiano,
    grated
handful of flat-leaf parsley,
    finely chopped
sea salt
freshly ground black pepper
freshly grated nutmeg
knob of butter

Guy's mother used to cook this warm and soothing broth when her children weren't feeling well, and Guy always thought it made him feel better.

Bring the chicken stock to the boil in a saucepan. Whisk the eggs, cheese and parsley in a bowl and season to taste with salt, pepper and nutmeg. Add to the stock – the egg will cook almost instantly. Leave to set for a moment, then lightly stir with a fork so the egg separates into strands (if you do this too soon, the strands will be small and will make the soup look grainy). Gently stir in the butter and serve immediately.

Serves 4

'*Gallina vecchia fa buon brodo.* (An old chicken makes good soup.)'

RISOTTO CON SALSICCIA, VINO ROSSO E PISELLI

RISOTTO WITH SAUSAGE, RED WINE AND PEAS

FROM ALESSANDRO PAVONI

olive oil

200 g Italian sausages, meat removed from the casings and chopped

300 g peas

90 g butter

200 g parmigiano reggiano, grated

6 litres chicken stock

400 ml red wine

large pinch of saffron threads

2 onions, chopped

1 garlic clove, finely chopped

1 small red chilli, finely chopped

1 kg carnaroli rice

handful of flat-leaf parsley, finely chopped

salt and pepper

Here's some risotto vocabulary. As you toast the rice grains in oil before adding the wine and stock, that's called the '*tostatura*'. When the rice has swollen to al dente, it is rested for a minute and then the butter and parmesan are added – this is the '*mantecatura*'. And when you have achieved the perfect consistency – when the risotto moves around with the spoon like a rippling wave – that's called '*all'onda*' (the wave).

This large risotto is perfect for feeding a crowd.

Heat a splash of oil in a frying pan and brown the sausage. Drain on paper towel.

Blanch two-thirds of the peas, then drain and puree them with a little of the butter and parmigiano reggiano. Set aside.

Heat the stock in a pot. Heat the wine with the saffron in a separate saucepan. Meanwhile, heat 80 ml of olive oil in another pot and add the onion, garlic and chilli. Cook gently for about 8 minutes, until soft but not coloured. Add the rice and stir to toast the grains evenly, being careful not to let them burn. Add the hot wine, but don't stir the rice – just shake the pot. When the rice has absorbed the wine, begin adding stock about 300 ml at a time and allow it to absorb without stirring.

After 3–4 minutes, stir in the sausage. Keep adding stock without stirring for another 12 minutes. (You can use the spoon to check that the rice isn't sticking to the bottom of the pot.)

Stir in the pea puree and whole peas and cook for another 2 minutes, adding stock as needed, until the rice is al dente. Remove from the heat and stir in the parsley and remaining butter and parmigiano reggiano. Taste for seasoning.

Serves 10

BRODO — THE CURER OF ALL ILLS

For any calamity in Italian life, there is one main cure – a golden broth with seemingly magical properties. 'For a death, a failed exam or a broken heart, my mother would always make *brodo*,' remembers Rosa Matto. 'Chicken, quail or pigeon broth, with or without *pastina* [little pasta], is still my family's pana-cea for all ills. My adult children still request *brodo* from my mother's hands when they are miserable for whatever reason!'

Robert Castellani was taught that the best *brodo* has 'yellow eyes': 'To pre-pare family recipes, we would have chicken broth on the stove continuously. My father, Jack, was the cook at home; my mother was the wage-earner. When you made your brodo, it would have chicken bones, shin bones and lots of vegetables. A good-quality *brodo* was one which had the fat still on top – it was described as having 'yellow eyes' on top. Mmmmm, *bello, bello, bello!'*

ARANCINI

FROM GUY GROSSI

VEAL RAGU
2½ tablespoons olive oil
1 onion, diced
1 garlic clove, finely chopped
1 carrot, diced
1 celery stalk, diced
200 g minced veal
sea salt
freshly ground black pepper
4 tablespoons tomato paste
100 ml red wine
400 ml chicken stock

RISOTTO
splash of olive oil
60 g butter
1 small onion, diced
2 cups arborio rice
1 litre chicken stock, warmed
pinch of saffron threads
sea salt
freshly ground black pepper
80 g parmigiano reggiano,
    grated

500 ml olive oil for deep-
    frying
plain flour
3 eggs, lightly beaten
3 cups dried breadcrumbs

These classic risotto balls with a filling of veal ragu (you can also fill them with small pieces of mozzarella) are a great antipasto. The only problem is they're so delicious, it's easy to eat a few too many before the meal!

To make the veal ragu, heat the olive oil in a saucepan over medium heat and fry the onion and garlic until the onion is translucent. Add the carrot and celery and fry until soft. Add the veal and stir until well browned. Taste for salt and pepper, then add the tomato paste and cook for a few minutes. Add the wine and simmer for 2–3 minutes, then add the stock. Reduce the heat and simmer gently for 45 minutes, stirring occasionally. The ragu should be thick. Remove from the heat and allow to cool.

To make the risotto, heat the olive oil and half the butter in a heavy-based saucepan over medium heat. Add the onion and fry until translucent. Add the rice and sauté for 1–2 minutes, then pour in the warm chicken stock. Add the saffron and season to taste with salt and pepper. Reduce the heat and simmer, covered with a lid, and stirring from time to time, until the rice is cooked (about 20 minutes). Finish by stirring in the parmigiano reggiano and the remaining butter until well combined. Pour into a shallow dish and set aside to cool.

To make the arancini balls, take a heaped tablespoon of risotto and roll it in the palm of your hand to form a ball. Push a hole in one side and fill with a teaspoon of ragu. Seal the hole and roll again, ensuring the ragu is completely enclosed. Continue making balls with the remaining risotto and ragu.

Heat the olive oil in a large saucepan or deep-fryer until very hot. Roll the balls in flour, then egg, and then breadcrumbs, and fry in batches for about 4 minutes until golden. Drain on paper towel and serve immediately.

Makes 24 arancini

TRIPPA STUFATA CON PINOLI E SULTANINA

SLOW-COOKED TRIPE WITH PINE NUTS AND SULTANAS

FROM GUY GROSSI

1 tablespoon olive oil
1 onion, sliced
2 garlic cloves, sliced
1 long red chilli, seeded and
    finely chopped
handful of basil leaves,
    crushed to a paste with
    olive oil
1 carrot, cut into batons
2 celery stalks, cut into batons
½ teaspoon freshly grated
    nutmeg
4 cloves, crushed
1 kg parboiled honeycomb ox
    tripe, cut into thin strips
1 tablespoon tomato paste
250 ml white wine
approximately 2 litres chicken
    stock or water
sea salt
freshly ground black pepper
generous handful of flat-leaf
    parsley, chopped
handful of pine nuts
handful of sultanas
freshly grated parmigiano
    reggiano

Tripe is one of those things people seem to either love or hate. Guy says he is the lucky one, as he grew up loving it. This is how he always cooks it – in a braise lightly flavoured with tomato.

Heat the oil in a pot and fry the onion, garlic and chilli until the onion is translucent. Stir in the basil paste followed by the carrot and celery and cook for about 5 minutes. Add the nutmeg, cloves and tripe and sauté briefly before adding the tomato paste. Stir constantly for a few minutes, until the tomato paste deepens in colour. Pour in the wine and let it reduce slightly, then add enough stock or water to cover the tripe. Season with salt and pepper and stir through three-quarters of the parsley. Simmer for 1–1½ hours.

To finish, stir through the pine nuts, sultanas and remaining parsley. Serve with parmigiano reggiano.

Serves 6

'*Sacco vuoto non sta in piedi.*
(An empty sack cannot stand, so eat up!)'

COTOLETTE

FROM ANNE GARREFFA

1 loaf of Italian bread,
   3 days old, crust removed,
   cut into chunks
4 garlic cloves
2 cups flat-leaf parsley leaves
100 g parmigiano reggiano,
   grated
dried chilli flakes to taste
   (optional)
12 thin slices of yearling
   beef girello
2–3 eggs
plain flour
good-quality salt
freshly ground black pepper
extra-virgin olive oil

Cotolette are like Italian schnitzels, and Anne's recipe includes garlic, parsley and parmesan in the breadcrumb coating. They are delicious served warm or cold with vegetables or salad, or you could do as Anne sometimes does and bake the *cotolette* layered up with a simple tomato and capsicum sauce, topped with extra breadcrumbs – the cotolette absorb the sauce and the dish is perfect taken along to a picnic a day or two later.

Put the bread in a food processor and process briefly until roughly chopped. Add the garlic and parsley and process until well combined. Add the parmigiano reggiano and chilli (if using) and process to fine breadcrumbs. Transfer to a bowl.

Flatten the beef slices with the smooth side of a mallet as thinly as you can. Beat the eggs in a bowl until smooth. Put some flour in a separate bowl and season with salt and pepper.

Dust the beef slices with flour, shaking off the excess, then dip into the egg, and then into the breadcrumbs.

Heat some oil in a frying pan over medium heat and fry a few *cotolette* at a time. Cook on each side until golden (not too brown) then drain on paper towel. Stack the *cotolette* on top of each other with paper towel in between to keep them warm and moist.

Serve warm, or refrigerate and serve cold.

Serves 6

SALTIMBOCCA

FROM GUY GROSSI

6 slices of veal loin or fillet
6 sage leaves
3 prosciutto slices, cut in half
40 g (¼ cup) plain flour
2 tablespoons olive oil
freshly ground black pepper
sea salt
splash of dry white wine
2 tablespoons stock
1 tablespoon butter
1 tablespoon chopped
   flat-leaf parsley

Beat the veal slices with the flat side of a mallet to an even thickness. Place a sage leaf on each followed by a piece of prosciutto. Fold over the edges of the veal steaks just to enclose the sage and prosciutto and tap again with the mallet to keep closed. Lightly dust the steaks with flour.

Heat the olive oil in a heavy-based frying pan and add the steaks, prosciutto-side down. Gently fry until golden. Sprinkle with pepper and a touch of salt and turn the steaks over. Deglaze the pan with the wine, then add the stock. Continue to cook the steaks for a few minutes, then remove from the pan. Add the butter and parsley to the pan and heat briefly to form a sauce. Spoon over the steaks and serve.

Serves 6

'*A cucina sana e svelta non occorre tanta scelta.* (Fast, healthy cooking does not need a lot of ingredients.)'

ABBACCHIO ALLA ROMANA

WET ROAST OF SUCKLING LAMB

FROM GUY GROSSI

1 suckling lamb weighing
6–8 kg, boned by your
butcher apart from the
saddle, which should be
cut into chops
1 onion, finely chopped
2 garlic cloves,
roughly chopped
1 long red chilli,
roughly chopped
3 ripe tomatoes,
roughly chopped
handful of flat-leaf parsley,
finely chopped, plus
extra to garnish
2 rosemary sprigs, leaves
picked and finely chopped
sprig of sage, leaves picked
and finely chopped
sprig of basil, leaves picked
and pounded to a paste
with olive oil
sea salt
freshly ground black pepper
750 ml dry white wine
375 ml extra-virgin olive oil
1½ cups freshly grated
parmigiano reggiano
1½ cups fresh breadcrumbs

Trim the lamb meat of excess skin and fat and cut into 4 cm chunks.

Preheat the oven to 180°C. Place the diced lamb and chops on a large tray and scatter with the onion, garlic, chilli, tomato and herbs, including the basil paste. Season with salt and pepper. Toss the lamb with the ingredients to coat evenly. Pour over the wine and oil, and add enough water to cover the meat. Sprinkle the parmigiano reggiano and breadcrumbs on top.

Roast in the oven for 40 minutes, until the crust is golden. Sprinkle with more parsley and serve with crusty bread to mop up the juices.

Serves 12

*'Il diavolo fa le pentole ma non i coperchi.
(The devil makes the pots but not the lids,
meaning your mistakes will be revealed.)'*

SUNDAY LUNCH

One of the cardinal rules of Italian life is Sunday is family day. And of course, in a country that's predominantly Catholic, it's God's day too. Families gather, sometimes up to four generations at a time. And eat. There's no question that you'd want to be anywhere else but with your family on Sunday. Even if you're young and sporting designer sunglasses, you'll be there – although you might go out to meet friends afterwards.

'We all had to be at the table for Sunday lunch without fail,' remembers gelato-maker Salvatore La Rosa. 'And then on Sunday evenings we all worked together to make biscuits and sausages.'

At the Castellani household, it was Nonna's job to tell her grandson Robert, now a chef, that he needed to eat more. 'She would always say to us, particularly me as I was growing up being a bean-pole, to "*mangia* [eat]". She would always say in a very high pitched voice, "You too skinny, *mamma mia. Mangia filio, mangia*! [Eat son, eat!]" She would also say that I would have to eat red meat because red meat made red blood.'

Red meat is often the centrepiece of a Sunday lunch or family feast. It could be a shoulder of veal cooked slowly over a spit, its flesh studded with garlic and lemon wedges, anointed with olive oil. Vince Garreffa talks about this being a feast in his family in the days when families got by on very little.

Families from Abruzzo get together with their favourite spit roast – *porchetta* – often a whole pig, boned and cooked with herbs and spices until the outside is golden and crackling, and the inside tender and full of flavour.

And if you're from Florence, you'd probably be tucking in to a good *bistecca*, an enormous T-bone steak cooked over charcoal. Authentic Florentine steak comes from cattle that existed in Roman times – big, beautiful beasts called Chianina, from the Chiana Valley in Tuscany, which grow very big with long legs. The cattle are slow growing and their meat develops great depth of flavour after they reach the age of two years.

To grow these cattle requires special fences, 'otherwise they will jump and visit next door's property and so on to the next. The grass – it's always greener next door, even for a cow!' laughs Salvatore Pepe, a chef who has mastered the art of cooking these amazing steaks.

'My friend ten years ago tried to raise four Chianina, which he brought with him from Italy and left at his property,' says Salvatore. 'They disappeared within a few weeks. He thought they got stolen but he was wrong. Someone found them many months later jumping from one property to the next!'

Guy Grossi remembers countless Sunday lunches with his family, and the glorious aftermath – leftovers. 'There are always lots of leftovers – lots and *lots* of leftovers because there is always that generosity and always, always, way too much,' he says. 'I still do that; we never get it right. I always think next time we'll just make a little bit less, but because you want everybody to have a little bit of everything, you always make more than enough!'

CARPACCIO

FROM GUY GROSSI

200 g beef fillet or sirloin
1 egg yolk
juice of 1 lemon
sea salt
freshly ground black pepper
100 ml extra-virgin olive oil
handful of radicchio leaves,
    finely shredded
parmigiano reggiano

This is a modern rendition of a classic Italian dish. A friend gave the recipe to Guy's family in the 1960s and it has evolved from there. The dish depends on the purity of the produce – really great, fresh beef, beaten out very thinly, and really good olive oil – and on keeping it simple. Guy adds radicchio and parmesan.

Slice the beef as finely as possible and place the slices between 2 layers of plastic wrap. Pound with the flat side of a meat mallet from the middle outwards, until very thin and almost translucent. Remove the top layer of plastic and turn the meat onto a cold plate.

Whisk the egg yolk, lemon juice and salt and pepper in a bowl. Add the olive oil a little at a time (you may not need all of it), whisking until emulsified and slightly thickened.

Dress the radicchio with an extra splash of oil and scatter over the beef. Season with salt. Shave some parmigiano reggiano over the top and drizzle with the lemon dressing.

Serves 4

'The person who talks at the table and whistles in bed is a stupid donkey. (This sounds better in Italian!)' Rosa Matto

VITELLO TONNATO
VEAL WITH TUNA SAUCE

FROM GUY GROSSI

VEAL
olive oil
1 kg young veal girello, trimmed of all sinew (trimmings reserved)
½ onion, roughly chopped
1 celery stalk, roughly chopped
½ carrot, roughly chopped
sprig of rosemary
2 bay leaves
handful of flat-leaf parsley, chopped
4 anchovy fillets
250 ml chardonnay vinegar
250 ml white wine
1 clove
handful of juniper berries
approximately 1 litre chicken stock
sea salt
freshly ground black pepper
juice of 1 lemon

TUNA SAUCE
5 eggs, hardboiled
500 g good-quality tinned tuna
100 g baby capers
juice of 1 lemon
250 ml extra-virgin olive oil
sea salt
freshly ground black pepper

GARNISH
baby capers
1–2 lemons, trimmed of peel and pith and cut into segments
rocket
shaved parmigiano reggiano
chopped flat-leaf parsley

People think vitello tonnato is so much work. Well it is, agrees Guy, but it's also one of the most beautiful and classic dishes of Italian cucina. It's festive and tastes superb when made well.

Heat a little oil in a frying pan and seal the veal on all sides until lightly golden. Transfer to a plate.

Pour a little more oil into the pan and add the veal trimmings, vegetables and herbs. Cook until the trimmings are well browned.

Transfer the mixture to a saucepan and add the anchovies, vinegar, wine, clove, juniper berries and the veal girello. Add enough stock to cover the veal. Season with salt and pepper. Simmer for 20–30 minutes, until the veal is just cooked. (To check, remove to a plate and insert a skewer – the juices should run clear.)

Once the veal is removed, boil the stock until reduced by half. Stir in the lemon juice then strain the stock through a fine sieve and allow to cool.

To make the sauce, puree the eggs and tuna in a blender, then add the capers and lemon juice and blend briefly. Slowly add the oil with the machine going, then slowly add enough cooled veal stock to make a creamy sauce a little thinner than mayonnaise.

Slice the cooled veal as thinly as you can. Spread half the sauce over the bottom of a serving dish and cover with the veal slices. Spread with the remaining sauce.

To serve, garnish each helping with about 4 baby capers, 2 lemon segments, 3 rocket leaves, some shaved parmigiano reggiano and a sprinkle of parsley.

Serves 4–6 as an entree

ANATRA ARROSTO RIPIENA

STUFFED ROASTED DUCK

FROM PATRIZIA SIMONE

HERB OIL
1 bunch flat-leaf parsley, finely chopped

1 small bunch sage, leaves picked and finely chopped

4 large fennel sprigs, finely chopped

a few sprigs of rosemary, leaves picked and finely chopped

1 onion, finely chopped

8 garlic cloves, finely chopped

1 tablespoon salt

1 tablespoon freshly ground black pepper

olive oil

DUCK
1.8 kg duck

1 large or 2 small pig's ears, cleaned and removed of hair

1 pig's trotter

1 fennel sprig

1 garlic clove, peeled

salt

100 g duck liver, soaked in salted water for a few hours

4 pork sausages

handful of boiled, peeled chestnuts, chopped (optional)

freshly ground black pepper

200 ml dry white wine such as pinot grigio

This is an old Umbrian recipe reserved for special occasions such as weddings and religious fetes. The stuffing is rich and rustic with braised pig's ear and trotter, duck liver, pork sausages and chestnuts, flavoured with herb oil. The leftover stuffing can be used to make duck-neck sausage.

To make the herb oil, put the herbs, onion, garlic, salt and pepper in a bowl and cover with oil. Mix well.

To make the stuffing for the duck, put the pig's ears, trotter, fennel sprig, garlic clove and some salt in a pot and cover with water. Bring to the boil, then reduce to a simmer and cook for 45 minutes. Remove the pig's ear and continue cooking the trotter for another hour. Drain and leave to cool.

Bring a saucepan of water to the boil and add the duck liver, blanching for 2 minutes. Drain and leave to cool.

Roughly chop the pig's ear and liver and put into a bowl. Remove the meat from the trotter bone, roughly chop it and add to the bowl. Remove the sausage meat from the casings and crumble into the bowl. Add the chestnuts if using, and 80 ml of the herb oil. If the mixture seems too dry, add some olive oil. Leave for 1 hour, or overnight, to allow the flavours to infuse.

Preheat the oven to 220°C. Wash the duck inside and out and pull off the excess fat. Cut off the neck (which you can use to make duck-neck sausage), but leave some skin to close over the cavity after stuffing the duck. Season the duck inside and out with salt and pepper and rub with herb oil.

Fill the cavity of the duck with the stuffing, being careful not to overfill it. Thread a wooden skewer through the skin at both ends to seal in the stuffing.

Lay the duck breast-side up on a tray and rub the breasts with a little more herb oil, being careful not to add too much as the herbs can burn in the oven. Add the wine and some water to the tray and cover the duck with foil. Roast in the oven for 1 hour, then remove the foil, reduce the temperature to 200°C and roast for approximately another hour, until cooked through (test by pulling out a leg and looking into the joint – the meat should no longer be pink and the juices should run clear).

Cut the duck into pieces and serve the stuffing on the side.

Serves 6

OUR SUNDAY FAMILY LUNCH
From Vince Gareffa, proud Calabrian and host of a lifetime of Sunday feasts

On the surface, it's a meal that everyone in the family must attend. But it's so much more than mere attendance – ever so subtly, what is happening would send psychiatrists to bankruptcy.

Family members are saying hello and catching up – having the time not only to exchange greetings, but to listen to the answers and engage in caring dialogue. Someone needs compassion; someone else guidance; another still, some love. 'I've missed you so much' and 'How are you?' – Mum's eyes would open big and bright when she set eyes on each of us. The old man – Pappa – stoic and blokey: 'Hey son, I've got to prune this tree. Give me a hand will you?' Bonding, sharing, caring.

Who's here, who's not? Let's ring them!
How are you coping with the baby?
I've got Wednesdays free if you want a break!
Here, I made some olives, take some! I've got too much parsley!
My dog is in heaven, I miss him so much … I know how you feel.
Don't forget his birthday next week.
Go and see a doctor, that looks bad.
What do you mean I have to apologise?!
Aunty helped me out.
My brother makes the best pizza!
Everyone invites me – I'm a good eater!

People don't go easily unnoticed at a Sunday family lunch. Oh yeah, and the food's good too!

VEAL OSSO BUCO WITH ANCHOVY GREMOLATA

FROM NINO ZOCCALI

4 thick slices of veal osso
buco weighing 350–450 g
each
sea salt
freshly ground black pepper
100 ml extra-virgin olive oil
2 medium–large onions,
finely diced
2 garlic cloves, finely chopped
2 good-quality anchovy fillets
2 large thyme sprigs
2 large sage sprigs
large sprig of rosemary
1 bay leaf
250 ml dry white wine
1 kg tomatoes, peeled,
seeded and crushed
250 ml veal stock

GREMOLATA
2 garlic cloves, finely chopped
2 tablespoons finely chopped
flat-leaf parsley
2 tablespoons finely chopped
good-quality anchovy fillets

Osso buco uses one of the top braising cuts from a veal or beef carcass – the shank or shin, which is cut into thick slices through the bone. Nino likes to use the best veal he can find, such as White Rocks Veal from Western Australia. 'The natural intra-muscular connective tissue turns into an amazing jelly as the meat cooks and develops such a wonderful flavour,' says Nino.

The meat is braised in a rich tomato sauce and the dish itself has become an Italian classic. For a luxurious meal indeed, serve it with saffron risotto.

Season the osso buco pieces with salt and pepper. Heat half the olive oil in a heavy-based saucepan that is wide enough to fit the osso buco pieces in one layer. Add to the pan and brown the pieces on each side. Remove to a plate and set aside.

Heat the remaining olive oil in the pan and add the onion, garlic, anchovies and herbs and gently sauté for 5 minutes, until the onion is translucent. Turn up the heat and deglaze the pan with the wine. Cook until the wine is almost completely reduced, then add the crushed tomatoes and veal stock. Bring to the boil, then reduce to a simmer and return the osso buco to the pan. Taste for seasoning and adjust accordingly – if the tomatoes are not as ripe and sweet at they could be, you might like to add a little sugar. Simmer gently for 2½–4 hours, covered with a lid, until the meat has begun to separate from the bone.

Combine the ingredients for the gremolata. Scatter over the osso buco and cover with the lid for 5 minutes. Lift the pieces of osso buco onto plates and spoon the sauce around the meat.

Serves 4

'Voglio sentire le cipolle gridere!
(Sauté the onions until you
hear them scream!)'

SALT-CRUSTED
SUCKLING LAMB

FROM ROBERT MARCHETTI

1 suckling lamb weighing
about 6 kg, legs and saddle
separated by your butcher,
and legs tunnel-boned
down to the shank
(shank bones left in)
½ cup sea salt
(preferably Sicilian)
½ cup sweet paprika
extra-virgin olive oil
6 punnets baby mache
(lamb's lettuce), or
watercress if unavailable,
leaves picked, washed
and dried
small piece of fresh
horseradish
(or 1 tablespoon
horseradish paste)
balsamic vinegar

This dish sings of family, says Robert Marchetti. 'And of sharing. In my home we cook this at Easter time … You can only eat so many painted boiled eggs.'

If you have a fan-forced oven, preheat it to 250°C. For a non fan-forced, preheat it to 270°C.

Combine the salt and paprika with enough oil to form a thick paste. Rub the paste all over the pieces of lamb, covering them thoroughly. Place the front legs and saddle on a wire rack set over a large tray, and the hind legs on a second rack set over a large tray.

Roast the lamb in the oven for 15 minutes or until a golden crust has formed. Turn the temperature down to 165°C for fan-forced, or 185°C for non fan-forced, and cook for a further 10–15 minutes. To check if the front legs and saddle are cooked, insert a skewer into the thickest part of the meat then remove it to see if the juices run clear. If so, remove the front legs and saddle from the oven. If not, leave in the oven with the hind legs and cook for a further 10–15 minutes, then check all the meat again. When all the meat is cooked, remove from the oven and leave to rest for about 30 minutes.

Meanwhile, put the mache leaves in a bowl and grate the horseradish over the top. Add a little extra-virgin olive oil and a small splash of balsamic vinegar (if using horseradish paste, mix it with the vinegar first). Toss together.

Slice the warm lamb, place on a serving plate and top with the salad.

Serves 12

BISTECCA ALLA FIORENTINA
FLORENTINE T-BONE STEAK

FROM SALVATORE PEPE

1 hand-cut Chianina T-bone
steak weighing 1.2–1.8 kg,
aged for 4–5 weeks
sea salt
extra-virgin olive oil

A true Florentine steak uses Chianina beef, and is always served rare. The steaks are enormous and designed to be shared.

Chianina is a large, muscular, slow-growing breed of cattle from the Chiana Valley in Italy. They were the oxen used to pull ploughs in the days of the Romans. Their meat is full flavoured, deeply coloured and surprisingly lean and tender – so tender you can eat it with a spoon.

Bring the steak to room temperature.

Light some coals in a charcoal grill and when the flames die down, evenly spread out the hot coals. Clean the grill with a steel brush and a dry cloth.

Grill the steak for 4–5 minutes on each side. The steak should be cooked rare.

Place on a serving platter, sprinkle with generous sea salt, drizzle with abundant olive oil, and serve immediately.

Serves 2–3

'La migliore carne è quella vicino all'osso. (The best meat is close to the bone.)'

SLOW-ROASTED VEAL WITH LEMON AND GARLIC

FROM VINCE GARREFFA

2 large lemons
1 boned veal shoulder
2 young garlic plants
   (spring onion-sized), sliced
   including the shoot, or
   4 finely sliced garlic cloves
   if unavailable
good-quality salt
freshly ground black pepper
extra-virgin olive oil
12 young lemon leaves
white wine

Butcher Vince Garreffa uses top-quality veal from Western Australia, as well as local organic salt. The veal shoulder is studded with juicy lemon wedges and sliced young garlic and rolled up with fragrant lemon leaves.

Preheat the oven to 120°C. Grate the zest of the lemons, then use a small, sharp knife to cut off the peel. Hold the lemons over a bowl to catch any juice and cut on either side of each segment to remove wedges of flesh, leaving the membranes behind. Leave the juice for another purpose.

Open the veal shoulder and cut slits 2 cm deep at 3 cm intervals across the inside of the shoulder (you should cut about 10 slits in total). Put some garlic and a lemon segment in each slit. Season with salt and pepper, scatter with the lemon zest and spread with the remaining lemon segments.

Roll up the shoulder encasing all your work and secure with butcher's string. Rub the outside of the shoulder with oil and season with salt and pepper. Slip the lemon leaves under the string spaced out across the shoulder. Place on a tray and roast for 4 hours.

Rest for 30 minutes before slicing. In the meantime, deglaze the roasting tray with a little white wine and reduce to make a sauce.

Serves 8–10

'The Italian table is about generosity and always, always way too much food.'

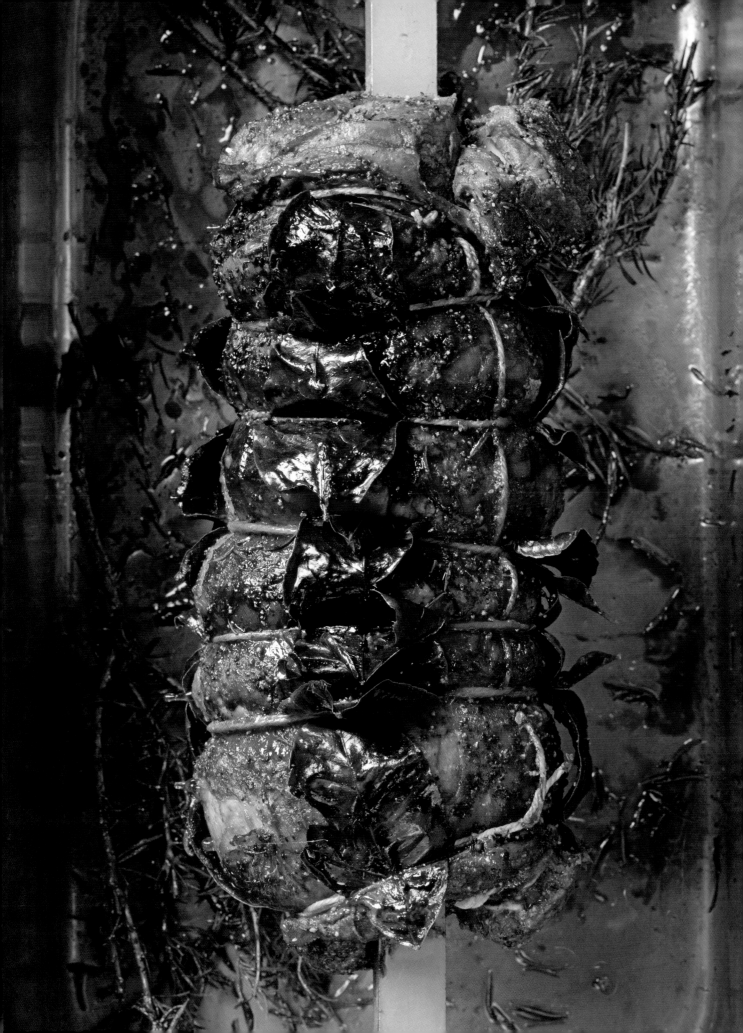

PORCHETTA

FROM GUY GROSSI

STUFFING
1 small stale loaf of bread,
   roughly chopped
1 bunch flat-leaf parsley,
   roughly chopped
3 garlic cloves
1 long red chilli
200 g parmesan, grated
2 eggs
150 ml olive oil

2 kg pork loin with skin
   attached
sea salt
freshly ground black pepper
1 onion, roughly chopped
1 carrot, roughly chopped
1 celery stalk, roughly
   chopped
150 ml olive oil
rosemary sprigs

Traditional roasted *porchetta* uses a whole side of pork and is cooked on a spit, but this recipe for pork loin is perfect for a home oven.

To make the stuffing, put the bread, parsley, garlic and chilli in a food processor and process to breadcrumbs. Add the parmesan, eggs and oil and process until well combined.

Preheat the oven to 200°C. Carefully slice off the skin of the pork loin, leaving one end attached. Open up the pork and season the flesh all over with salt and pepper. Cover the meat with the stuffing. Roll the meat around the stuffing, then roll the skin around the meat in the other direction. Tie with butcher's string.

Put the onion, carrot and celery on an oven tray. Place the pork on top and drizzle with the oil. Season the pork skin with salt, pepper and sprinkle with rosemary. Add enough water to the tray to just cover the vegetables. Roast the pork in the oven for 40 minutes.

Serves 8

Before a big meal we say, '*Pancia mia fatti capanna*'. (Make a house in my stomach for all this food.)

SWEETS

In Italy, *dolci* – sweets – are not something to end a meal, but are traditionally reserved for special occasions and feasts. Families look forward to Easter and Christmas and the beautiful treats only served at these times of year.

Memories of growing up in Italy are punctuated with delicious sweet moments. Adelina Pulford, a chef who now specialises in sweets, says she can remember the exquisite flavours of sweets eaten in her childhood as they were so rare. 'The most memorable Italian dessert would have to be *cannoli*,' she says. The filling she loved as a child and still does 'is a sublime mixture of ricotta, mascarpone, glacé orange peel, pistachios and sugar. The best way to describe it is a soft, fragrant crunch in my mouth followed by an explosion of creamy, nutty, orange flavour that sadly ends too soon. The remedy is to eat another one and try to eat a little slower if possible!'

Adelina's family, like many others in Italy, cooked on a gas ring and a wood fire, so most of their sweets were fried. 'At Easter it would be this pastry wrapped around an egg; it was called, in Calabrian dialect, "*pupulicchio*". At Christmas, it would be *scalille*, *chinulille*, *turdilli* and so on. All these sweets were fried either over the fire or the gas. On reflection, they were very time consuming.'

While Italians save their best sweets for special occasions, it's not to say that they don't enjoy sweets more regularly. Simple biscuits, cakes and pastries are eaten with coffee through the day rather than being formalised as 'dessert'. (For meals themselves, they prefer three or four savoury courses.)

Guy Grossi remembers the sweets that were part of his childhood. 'Mum would make biscotti or some sort of cake which would sit on the sideboard and get eaten slowly through the day – even for breakfast. You may have a biscotti with coffee or just on its own. You might have a slice of *torta* in the afternoon. It would just … disappear.'

Salvatore La Rosa has a similar memory. 'Our family would make Sicilian-style shortbread, which were ideal for dunking in milk or the drink our mother made us for breakfast every day – zabaglione, made from marsala, egg yolks and sugar.'

For pastry chef Loretta Sartori, the fried strips of pastry called *crostoli* that are traditionally made at Easter hold a special place in her heart. '*Crostoli* are served prior to the beginning of Lent – the Catholic practice of going without or making a small sacrifice during the forty days leading up to Easter Sunday,' she says. 'Let's face it – Italy is a Catholic nation, but like most Catholics, theory and practice go out the window, hence you can find a supply of *crostoli* all year round. Why wait until Easter? The trouble with *crostoli* is that they are rather labour intensive – all that cutting and frying once the dough has passed through the pasta machine – however, the result is simply scrumptious and the discipline to stop at one or two is rare to find. For this reason, we try to avoid making them frequently!

'The funny thing about the *crostoli* recipe (it's like the family sauce recipe – *sugo*), is everyone's mother makes the *best* one! I always offer my services to try everyone's mother's efforts in order to determine whose I prefer. The recipe must always include grappa – generally bootleg made in the family or some obscure uncle's still – or brandy, or a liqueur.'

'*Cin cin Cinzano! Fegato sano!*
(A little alcohol (Cinzano)
makes a healthy liver!)'
A favourite toast of Rosa Mitchell's father

Italians leave some sweets to the professionals rather than making them at home, and there are temples dedicated to these sweets – gleaming and filled with heavenly creations. '*Paste*' is a selection of cakes purchased from a *pasticceria*, which is generally given as a gift when people go out visiting. In Italy it is common practice to go to the local cake shop after church to purchase cakes to take along to the family you are having lunch with.

Marianna di Bartolo makes a range of wicked pastries and world-class nougat, and once worked at a *pasticceria* in Marostica, Veneto. 'I fully understood why Italians are so passionate about food and have extensive knowledge of it,' she says. 'Each weekend the children would choose the cakes that were to be purchased. As a result, their familiarity with the product, of what it comprised and the correct name, was reinforced … This applies to all food purchasing in Italy, so the children are educated into the cuisine.'

Marianna lists her great discoveries from that time:

Diplomatico: Two layers of puff pastry sandwiched with *crema* (custard – *crème pâtissière*) and sponge cake soaked in alchermes, which is a floral and spicy red liqueur.

Bigne: Choux pastry puffs filled with vanilla or chocolate *crema* and decorated with fondant icing.

Cannoli: Fried tubes of pastry filled with vanilla or chocolate *crema* or, in the Sicilian style, with ricotta and candied fruits.

Cannoncini: Puff-pastry horns filled with *crema*.

Pesche: Two domes of sponge cake sandwiched with *crema* and steeped in liqueur syrup, brushed with food colouring to look like a peach, and rolled in sugar.

Meringhe: Two light-as-a-feather meringues sandwiched with whipped cream. Layered sponge cakes sandwiched with *crema al buro* (butter cream) and liqueur sugar syrup …

'The list goes on,' Marianna says. 'No wonder I am a pastry chef!'

NONNA'S APPLE STRUDEL

FROM ROSETTA PIZZINI

PASTRY

185 ml milk

40 g butter

2 tablespoons sugar

300 g (2 cups)
   self-raising flour

2 medium eggs, beaten

FILLING

10 granny smith or red
   delicious apples, peeled,
   quartered, cored and
   thinly sliced

½ cup apricot jam

110 g (½ cup) sugar

100 g butter

½ cup currants

½ cup sultanas

ground cinnamon

ground cloves

Rosetta Pizzini is from Alto Adige in the Italian mountains near the Austrian border, and it shows in this recipe. Strudel is not seen as typically Italian, but Rosetta's sure hands as she made this was one of the most memorable images of the 'Italian Food Safari' series. The strudel is simply perfect, especially if you can source good homemade apricot jam.

To make the pastry, place the milk, butter and sugar in a saucepan and gently heat until the butter melts and the sugar dissolves.

Place the flour in a bowl, make a well in the centre and add the eggs and most of the milk mixture (leave a few tablespoons for a glaze). Stir until the mixture forms a ball, then transfer to a work surface and knead gently until smooth. The consistency should be a little softer than pasta dough. Cover with plastic wrap and refrigerate for 1 hour.

Preheat the oven to 180°C. Divide the dough into 3 pieces. Roll out the first piece on the floured work surface to an oval shape approximately 26 x 28 cm, and 5 mm thick. Spread the pastry with a third of the jam, going thinly to the edges. Spread a third of the apples over the pastry leaving a 2 cm edge free. Sprinkle with a third of the sugar and dot with a third of the butter. Scatter with a third of the currants and sultanas and sprinkle with cinnamon and cloves to your taste.

Fold the edges of the pastry over the filling to create a rim, and roll the strudel up from one of the long sides of the oval. Pick up the strudel with a couple of wide spatulas or egglifters and lay on a buttered tray. Follow the same process to make the next 2 strudels.

Glaze the strudels with the reserved milk mixture and bake them in the oven for 45 minutes. Baste them intermittently with the buttery syrup that oozes onto the trays to create shiny, golden pastry.

Serve with vanilla ice-cream or rich cream.

Makes 3 strudels to serve 12

RICOTTA CHEESECAKE

FROM LORETTA SARTORI

SHORTCRUST PASTRY
200 g unsalted butter, softened
100 g caster sugar
1 egg
300 g (2 cups) plain flour

FILLING
80 g almond meal
3 eggs
110 g (½ cup) sugar
350 g cream cheese at room temperature
650 g fresh ricotta
80 ml cream
80 g candied citrus peel, diced
100 g sultanas, soaked overnight in a little rum or brandy

icing sugar for dusting

To make the pastry, cream the butter and sugar with electric beaters until pale. Add the egg and continue beating until incorporated. Add the flour and beat just until combined. The dough will be very sticky. Cover in plastic wrap and refrigerate until you are ready to roll it out (leave for at least 30 minutes).

Preheat the oven to 180°C. Briefly knead the chilled dough to soften it, then roll it out on a lightly floured work surface. Place a 26 cm springform cake tin over the pastry and cut around the tin to give you a circle that will fit into the base. Set the tin aside and lift the circle of pastry onto a tray lined with baking paper. Bake the pastry for approximately 12 minutes, until golden. Allow the pastry to cool briefly.

Meanwhile, put the almond meal for the filling on another tray and lightly roast it in the oven.

Butter the cake tin and lay the baked pastry circle into the base. Cut strips of fresh pastry for the sides and press into the tin. Run your finger along the joins, including where the sides join to the base, to seal.

Beat the eggs with half the sugar until pale and frothy. Set aside.

Beat the cream cheese and remaining sugar until smooth, then add the ricotta and beat again until smooth. Beat in the cream, then gradually beat in the eggs. Fold in the almond meal, candied peel and sultanas. Spoon into the pastry base and bake in the oven for 1 hour.

Leave to cool to room temperature, remove from the tin and dust with icing sugar.

Serves 12

LA TORTA DELLA NONNA GARREFFA

FROM TONI ROMEO

SHORTCRUST PASTRY
250 g self-raising flour
125 g butter, softened
125 g sugar
1 egg
grated zest of 1 lemon

VANILLA CUSTARD
1½ tablespoons custard
    powder
1½ tablespoons sugar
350 ml milk
1 egg yolk

CHOCOLATE CUSTARD
1½ tablespoons custard
    powder
1½ tablespoons sugar
1½ tablespoons cocoa powder
350 ml milk
1 egg yolk

This recipe from Toni's mother is the most requested from the Italian Food Safari series – a wonderful tart (and simple to make, too) with layers of vanilla and chocolate custard.

To make the pastry, put the flour and butter in a bowl and rub with your fingers until the mixture resembles breadcrumbs. Add the sugar, egg and lemon zest and form into a dough. Refrigerate for 30 minutes.

Butter a deep 20 cm tart tin. Roll out the dough and lay it into the tin.

Preheat the oven to 180°C. To make the vanilla custard, place the custard powder and sugar in a saucepan and blend with some of the milk until smooth. Stir in the remaining milk and egg yolk and cook over low heat, stirring, until thickened.

Repeat the process to make the chocolate custard, adding the cocoa with the custard powder and sugar.

Pour the vanilla custard into the pastry base. Top with the chocolate custard. Bake in the oven for approximately 30 minutes, until the pastry is golden. Leave to cool before cutting and serving.

Serves 10

'To show you care, for special occasions, you make something by hand that takes time rather than choosing an easy dish.'

CANNOLI DI RICOTTA

FROM ACHILLE MELLINI

PASTRY
680 g plain flour
130 g (1 cup) icing sugar
160 g butter or lard, melted
2 eggs plus 3–4 egg yolks
250 ml marsala

FILLING
½ cup glacé cherries
1 teaspoon orange essence
1 teaspoon rum
300 g fresh ricotta
100 g caster sugar
200 g mascarpone
½ cup candied citrus peel
2 tablespoons chopped dark
    couverture chocolate

1 egg, beaten
sunflower oil for deep-frying
icing sugar for dusting

The day before, put the flour and icing sugar into a bowl and stir in the butter or lard. Add the eggs, egg yolks and marsala and mix together until it forms a dough. Transfer to a work surface and knead for a few minutes. (The dough can also be made in an electric mixer with a dough hook.) Cover in plastic wrap and refrigerate overnight.

Soak the glacé cherries in the orange essence and rum overnight.

The next day, beat the ricotta and sugar with electric beaters for 2 minutes until smooth. Beat in the mascarpone, then fold in the cherries, candied peel and chocolate. Chill the filling in the refrigerator.

Divide the dough into a few pieces so it is easier to work with. Roll the first piece through a pasta machine on the widest setting. Fold it in half and run it through the machine again. Do this several times until smooth, then start rolling it out at narrower settings until 1 mm thick. Lay the sheet on a floured surface while you roll out the other pieces of dough.

Cut the sheets into circles 10 cm in diameter and brush half of each circle with beaten egg. Wrap around metal cannoli tubes beginning from the side not brushed with egg. Use the egg to stick the edge of the circle down.

Deep-fry the *cannoli* in hot sunflower oil for 30 seconds, until golden brown. Drain on paper towel and remove the metal tubes.

Fill the *cannoli* just before serving and dust with icing sugar. Serve with orange ice-cream if desired.

Makes approximately 50 cannoli

CRESPELLE DI CASTAGNE CON MIELE, PIGNOLI E ROSEMARINO

CHESTNUT-FLOUR CREPES WITH HONEY, PINE NUTS AND ROSEMARY

FROM GUY GROSSI

handful of pine nuts
sprig of rosemary, leaves
    picked
110 g (¾ cup) plain flour
½ cup chestnut flour
1 tablespoon caster sugar
4 eggs, beaten
250 ml milk
1 tablespoon butter, melted
cottonseed or other
    mild-flavoured oil
chestnut-flower honey

This is a peasant dish that uses chestnut flour and chestnut-flower honey, a delicious, intense honey. Chestnut flour is used in many dishes in Italian cucina – another is a flat, almost savoury cake from Tuscany called *castagnaccio*, which is flavoured with olive oil, rosemary and pine nuts.

Gently toast the pine nuts and rosemary leaves in a dry frying pan. Set aside.

Mix the flours and sugar in a bowl, then make a well in the centre and add the eggs. Gradually whisk in the milk, then the butter. Leave the batter to rest for at least 20 minutes before cooking.

Gently heat a little oil in a small frying pan and pour in enough batter to coat the base of the pan. Cook the crepe for 1 minute, then turn and cook for 30 seconds on the other side. Slide onto a plate and keep warm while you continue making crepes with the remaining batter.

To serve, drizzle each crepe with honey, then fold in half and drizzle again. Fold into quarters and garnish with pine nuts and rosemary.

Serves 6

'You embrace your family history through your family recipes.'

ZABAGLIONE

FROM GUY GROSSI

4 egg yolks
100 g caster sugar
125 ml marsala
125 ml white wine

Guy's mum used to make zabaglione for her children in the morning before sending them off to school. It gives you a little kick of energy, and the marsala adds some zing. This old-fashioned custard makes a nice, light dessert.

Whisk the ingredients together in a large bowl. Place the bowl over a saucepan of simmering water and continue to whisk until warm, expanded in volume and forming soft peaks (approximately 10 minutes). Pour into glasses and serve.

Serves 4

'*La speranza è una buona colazione, ma una pessima cena.* (Hope makes a good breakfast but a bad supper.)

PANNACOTTA AL PROSECCO

PROSECCO PANNACOTTA

FROM ADELINA PULFORD

3 gelatine leaves
500 ml cream
75 g (⅓ cup) sugar
½ vanilla bean, seeds scraped
200 ml prosecco from a
    freshly opened bottle

BERRY SAUCE
200 g sugar
200 ml water
400 g fresh or frozen berries

fresh berries to garnish
mint leaves to garnish

Dessert queen Adelina Pulford was inspired to put two beautiful things together – elegant, sparkling prosecco wine and creamy, silky panna-cotta – while travelling in Piemonte, where she saw pannacotta being made with *spumante di asti*.

Lightly oil 8 dariole moulds (flexible plastic moulds are great for unmoulding) or ramekin dishes. Chill in the refrigerator.

Put the gelatine leaves in a bowl of cold water to soften. Meanwhile, softly whip half the cream in a bowl and set aside. Put the remaining cream, sugar and vanilla seeds in a saucepan and bring to a simmer, then remove from the heat.

Drain the gelatine, add to the hot cream and stir until dissolved. Pour the mixture into a bowl set over a large bowl of ice and stir until it has completely cooled and begun to thicken (5–10 minutes).

Gently fold in the whipped cream. Pop the cork on the prosecco and quickly fold in 200 ml. Pour into the moulds and refrigerate for at least 2 hours, until set.

For the berry sauce, put the sugar and water in a saucepan and heat, stirring, until the sugar dissolves. Add the berries. Transfer the mixture to a blender or food processor and puree. Strain through a fine sieve and chill in the refrigerator.

To serve, drizzle berry sauce onto plates in a decorative pattern. Remove the pannacottas from their moulds by either loosening with a palette knife or immersing briefly in warm water. Garnish with fresh berries and mint leaves.

Serves 8

'The best dishes are often cooked in the smallest pot.'

SEMIFREDDO CROCCANTE

PRALINE SEMIFREDDO

FROM GUY GROSSI

PRALINE
100 g flaked almonds, toasted
100 g sugar

SEMIFREDDO
80 g sugar
200 g honey
80 g liquid glucose
150 ml egg whites (from approximately 5 eggs)
900 ml cream

This is a great way to make an ice-cream dessert without using an ice-cream machine – you just put the semifreddo in the freezer. Guy likes to serve it with fresh berries or peaches in summer, or poached pears and chocolate sauce in winter.

To make the praline, scatter the almonds on a tray lined with baking paper. Melt the sugar in a saucepan over medium heat, then cook to a light caramel. Pour over the almonds and leave to cool, then crush the praline to a fine powder.

To make the semifreddo, put the sugar, honey and glucose in a saucepan and cook until the mixture reaches 125°C on a sugar thermometer. Remove from the heat and set aside until the mixture cools to 90°C.

While cooling, beat the egg whites to soft peaks. With the beaters running, gradually pour in the sugar mixture in a thin stream. Continue to beat until the mixture cools (about 5 minutes).

Lightly whip the cream, then fold the cream and crushed praline into the egg whites. Pour into a terrine mould or loaf tin lined with baking paper. Tap the mould gently to take the mixture to the corners, and smooth the top. Freeze overnight.

To serve, turn the semifreddo out of the mould and slice with a hot knife.

Serves 12

COFFEE

Italian coffee is an institution. It punctuates the day and gives a reason to get together and socialise, particularly for many older Italians who might drink up to five cups a day.

'If you're born Italian, you start your day with coffee,' explains coffee consultant Sam Cosentino. 'If you sent an Italian to a desert island and told them they could take three things, one of them would be an Italian stovetop cafeteria! Coffee is as embedded in Italian culture as pasta and bread.'

'We drink coffee from an early age,' explains Guy Grossi. 'It's the tradition at home – the little *machinetta* would sit on the stove and coffee would always be made after every meal. The machine would go on and of course Mum and Dad drank coffee, and as we got older we learnt to drink coffee too. In the morning the leftover coffee from the night before would be mixed with milk – half and half – and that would be warmed up and you'd get a big cup of it with some cake or something sweet to dip in. That was breakfast, and that's the original cafe latte – coffee and milk mixed together. We drank that from a very young age. Then as you grow up, you have your first cappuccino and the rest is history. Every Italian drinks coffee!'

Apart from coffee with milk in the morning, Italians generally drink their coffee black – in four ways according to Sam Cosentino:

Espresso: otherwise known as a 'short black'.
Ristretto: 'restricted' to 15–20 ml – a stronger, shorter coffee.
Corretto: 'corrected' with a dash of alcohol, usually grappa.
Macchiato: the word means to stain or mark the espresso, either with a slight dash of cold or hot milk or half a teaspoon of frothed milk.

The world has embraced Italian coffee and many people prefer it with milk, flouting the Italian rule of no coffee with milk after midday. Some commit even worse sins: 'I see people eating pasta with a cappuccino at their elbow!' grimaces Sam. 'In Naples, where good espresso coffee is a priority, they'd lock you up for three years for committing such a crime!'

Temperature is the other major factor for the true aficionado. Italian coffee should not be scalding, as it makes it impossible to taste the subtlety of its flavour.

No matter how you like your coffee, most people agree that coffee is the perfect partner to something sweet. Crisp little morsels of biscotti or exquisitely flaky shell-shaped *sfogliatelle* filled with ricotta – the Italians specialise in a vast array of pick-me-ups to have with coffee at any time of day.

'Sometimes the Italian national soccer team will not go on the field until they have had their espresso coffee!'

BISCOTTI

FROM ARMANDO PERCUOCO

600 g plain flour
600 g caster sugar
2 teaspoons baking powder
pinch of salt
100 g flaked almonds
100 g pistachios
1 vanilla bean, seeds scraped
grated zest of 2 oranges
grated zest of 2 lemons
grated zest of 2 limes
4 eggs plus 2 egg yolks
3 tablespoons pernod,
    sambucca or other
    liqueur of choice

You will want to make this wonderful recipe time after time. From chef Armando Percuoco, and made by his pastry chef Alessandra Rispoli, these biscotti are scented with orange, lemon, lime, vanilla and liqueur.

Put the flour, sugar, baking powder, salt, nuts, vanilla seeds and citrus zest in a large bowl and stir together. Add the eggs, egg yolks and liqueur and mix until well combined. Roll into logs around 4 cm wide and place on buttered trays. Refrigerate for 20 minutes. (You can refrigerate for longer if it suits – just wrap the logs with plastic wrap so they don't dry out.)

Preheat the oven to 180°C. Place the logs in the oven and bake for 10–15 minutes, until golden brown. Allow to cool.

Preheat the oven to 160°C. Thinly slice the logs, return the slices to the trays and bake for another 5 minutes. Be careful not to over bake the biscotti as they can become too hard. Store in an airtight container.

Makes 40 biscotti

In times of war, the Italians were renowned for making espresso coffee for soldiers regardless of what army they were in. Soldiers returned to houses just for the coffee, exchanging it for fresh eggs.

CROSTOLI

FROM VANESSA MARTIN

500 g plain flour
1 sachet of Lievito Bertolini
   (vanilla-flavoured raising
   agent), or 1 teaspoon baking
   powder and 1 teaspoon
   vanilla extract
3 tablespoons icing sugar,
   plus extra for dusting
grated zest of 1 orange
grated zest of 1 lemon
3 tablespoons unsalted butter,
   softened
1 tablespoon grappa
   (Italian brandy)
3 eggs
cottonseed oil for deep-frying

The food of the angels. Flavoured with citrus zest and grappa, and sprinkled with icing sugar, *crostoli* are the lightest ribbons of fried pastry and a must for every Italian gathering at Christmas, Easter and christenings. *Crostoli* are believed to originate from the Veneto region and this version is from Venetian-born chef Vanessa Martin.

Combine the flour, *Lievito* sachet (or baking powder and vanilla), icing sugar and citrus zest in a bowl. Rub in the butter until the mixture resembles breadcrumbs. (This can also be done in a food processor.) Add the grappa and eggs and mix with your hands to form a dough. Transfer to a work surface and knead for a few minutes. Cover in plastic wrap and leave to rest for 30 minutes.

Divide the dough into a few pieces so it is easier to work with. Roll the first piece through a pasta machine on the widest setting. Fold it in half and run it through the machine again. Do this several times until smooth, then start rolling it out at narrower settings until you reach the last setting and have a very thin, long sheet. Lay the sheet on a floured surface while you roll out the other pieces of dough.

Cut the sheets into strips 3–4 cm wide (a ravioli cutting wheel with a crimped edge gives a decorative look). Cut a few small slits in the centre of each strip running lengthways.

Deep-fry small batches of *crostoli* in hot oil (180°C) until pale golden. Drain on paper towel. Dust with icing sugar to serve.

Makes approximately 100 *crostoli*

'The Italian stovetop cafeteria (espresso maker) is still the most widely used brewing system in Italy – most homes have two or three.'

TIPS ON ENJOYING GREAT ITALIAN COFFEE
From Aldo Cozzi, coffee merchant

1. Buy fresh roasted coffee beans or ground coffee every two weeks.
2. Store coffee in the refrigerator – treat it as a fresh food.
3. For plunger coffee, add the coffee and then some cold water to just cover it before adding the hot water – this gives a much better flavour.
4. For a stovetop device, make sure the coffee is not too fine or too coarse – you should get a nice brown *crema* on top of your coffee.
5. Buy blended coffee rather than single origin – the taste is more complex and pleasing.

TIRAMISU

FROM GUY GROSSI

3 egg yolks
60 g caster sugar
500 g mascarpone
2 tablespoons Strega liqueur,
    or more to taste
1 tablespoon sambucca,
    or more to taste
20–30 *savoiardi* (sponge
    finger) biscuits
1 litre hot espresso coffee
100 g dark chocolate,
    chopped
freshly ground coffee beans

ITALIAN MERINGUE
100 ml water
250 g sugar
125 ml egg whites
    (from 4–5 eggs)

This is Guy Grossi's recipe made by chef Graziella Alessi – a masterpiece of Italian meringue (beaten egg whites stabilised with cooked sugar syrup), mascarpone and biscuits soaked in coffee, dusted with ground coffee beans.

Put the egg yolks and caster sugar in a mixing bowl and beat on high speed until pale and thick. Add the mascarpone and beat on medium speed until combined (be careful not to over mix as you may split the mascarpone). Add the Strega and sambucca and beat briefly. Set aside while you make the meringue.

Pour the water into a very clean, grease-free saucepan and slowly add the sugar, making sure all the grains get wet. Bring to the boil over medium heat and cook to soft-ball stage, which is when you can drop a small amount of syrup into cold water and it forms a ball that you can shape in your fingers. It is at 112°C on a sugar thermometer.

Beat the egg whites on high speed in a very clean bowl until they hold medium peaks. With the beaters still going, slowly add the hot syrup in a thin stream. Continue to beat until the meringue is completely cool.

Gently fold the meringue into the mascarpone mixture. Taste and add extra Strega and sambucca if desired.

Soak the *savoiardi* biscuits in the coffee a few at a time without letting them get completely sodden, and giving them a light squeeze as you take them out. (The coffee shouldn't soak all the way through, so there should still be a little portion of biscuit in the middle left untouched.) Lay the biscuits into a large bowl, and keep soaking and adding biscuits until you have lined the base and sides entirely.

Sprinkle the biscuits with a little of the chopped chocolate. Spread one third of the mascarpone mixture over the top. Cover with more coffee-soaked biscuits, sprinkle with more chocolate and add another third of mascarpone. Repeat the layers again and smooth the top.

Refrigerate for at least 2 hours, until the tiramisu is firm enough to cut. Just before serving, sprinkle with ground coffee.

Serves 10–12

SFOGLIATELLE

FROM CLAUDIO FERRARO

PASTRY
500 g plain flour
50 g sugar
6 g salt
200 ml water
150 g lard, softened

FILLING
900 ml water
130 g sugar, plus 60 g extra
6 g salt
310 g semolina
vegetable oil
1.3 kg fresh ricotta
2 eggs
grated zest of 1 orange
1 vanilla bean, seeds scraped
1 teaspoon ground cinnamon

These pastries are truly a combination of passion and skill. Flaky pastry is fashioned into shells and has a glorious crunch, with a creamy filling.

To make the pastry, put the flour, sugar and salt in a bowl and gradually mix in the water with your hands forming a stiff dough. Knead for a few minutes, cover with plastic wrap and leave to rest for about 30 minutes.

Divide the dough into a few pieces (each about the size of a slice of bread) so it is easier to work with. Take the first piece and roll it through a pasta machine on the widest setting. Fold it in three and run it through the machine again. Do this about 4 times until smooth, then start rolling the pasta out at narrower settings until the sheet is 1 mm thick. Lay the sheet on a work surface and use your fingers to paint with a layer of the lard.

Begin rolling the sheet up from one of the short edges, gently stretching it longer and wider as you do so, until you have formed a cigar. Then roll another piece of dough through the pasta machine, coat it with lard, and roll it up around the first sheet to create a thicker roll. Continue with the rest of the dough until you have formed a large roll. Cover with plastic wrap and refrigerate for at least 1 hour.

To make the filling, put the water, 130 g of sugar and salt in a saucepan and bring to the boil. Once boiling, gradually add the semolina, stirring. Cook for about 5 minutes, until thick. Remove from the heat, brush the top with a little vegetable oil and place the pan in the refrigerator to cool.

Remove the semolina from the saucepan, cut into small cubes and place in a bowl with the extra sugar. Beat with electric beaters until it breaks up. Add the ricotta and one of the eggs and continue beating until smooth. Add the remaining egg, orange zest, vanilla seeds and cinnamon and beat for another 3 minutes.

Preheat the oven to 180°C. Cut the chilled pastry into 1 cm slices with a serrated knife. Use your fingers to massage a little lard into the cut sides of each slice and gently push out the centre of the spiral, separating the layers to gradually form a pouch or shell. Scoop some ricotta mixture into the centre, filling to the top. Loosely close the shell and lay it on a tray lined with baking paper. Bake for 25–30 minutes, until crisp and golden.

Makes 20–25 sfogliatelle

An SBS Book

Published in 2010 by Hardie Grant Books

Hardie Grant Books (Australia)
85 High Street
Prahran, Victoria 3181
www.hardiegrant.com.au

Hardie Grant Books (UK)
Second Floor, North Suite
Dudley House
Southhampton Street
London WC2E 7HF
www.hardiegrant.co.uk

Cataloguing-in-Publication data is available from the National Library of Australia.

ISBN 9 781 742 700 007

Cover and text design by Pfisterer + Freeman
Studio food photography by Gorta Yuuki
Food styling by Simon Bajada
Location photography by Toufic Charabati
Additional location photography by Alan Benson and Oliver Strewe
Colour reproduction by Splitting Image Colour Studio
Printed and bound in China by C & C Offset Printing

The publishers would like to thank the following for their generosity in supplying props for the book: Market Import, Major & Tom, Shelley Panton Ceramics and Izzi & Popo.

10 9 8 7 6 5 4 3 2 1